Digital Painting fundamentals with Corel® Painter™ 12

Rhoda Grossman Draws

Course Technology PTR
A part of Cengage Learning

COURSE TECHNOLOGY
CENGAGE Learning™

Australia, Brazil, Japan, Korea, Mexico, Singapore, Spain, United Kingdom, United States

COURSE TECHNOLOGY
CENGAGE Learning™

**Digital Painting Fundamentals
with Corel® Painter™ 12
Rhoda Grossman Draws**

**Publisher and General Manager,
Course Technology PTR:**
Stacy L. Hiquet

Associate Director of Marketing:
Sarah Panella

Manager of Editorial Services:
Heather Talbot

Acquisitions Editor:
Megan Belanger

Marketing Manager:
Jordan Castellani

Marketing Development Manager:
Michelle Arcadipane

Project/Copy Editor:
Kezia Endsley

Technical Reviewer:
Barbara Pollack

Interior Layout:
Shawn Morningstar

Cover Designer:
Mike Tanamachi

Indexer:
Kelly Talbot Editing Services

Proofreader:
Kelly Talbot Editing Services

For product information and technology assistance,
contact us at

**Cengage Learning Customer & Sales Support,
1-800-354-9706**

For permission to use material from this text or product,
submit all requests online at **cengage.com/permissions**

Further permissions questions can be emailed to
permissionrequest@cengage.com

Library of Congress Control Number: 2011926542

ISBN-13: 978-1-4354-5988-5

ISBN-10: 1-4354-5988-1

Course Technology, a part of Cengage Learning
20 Channel Center Street
Boston, MA 02210
USA

Cengage Learning is a leading provider of customized learning solutions with office locations around the globe, including Singapore, the United Kingdom, Australia, Mexico, Brazil, and Japan. Locate your local office at:
international.cengage.com/region

Cengage Learning products are represented in Canada by Nelson Education, Ltd.

For your lifelong learning solutions, visit **courseptr.com**
Visit our corporate website at **cengage.com**

Printed in the United States of America
1 2 3 4 5 6 7 13 12 11

For my friends and colleagues at the Industrial Center Building in Sausalito, where I hang one of my many hats.

About the Author

Rhoda Draws, the artist formerly known as Rhoda Grossman, is the author of numerous books and video tutorials on the creative uses of Corel Painter and Adobe Photoshop. She began to transfer her traditional fine art, illustration, and cartooning skills to the computer 20 years ago. Based in the San Francisco Bay area, Rhoda draws and paints in a studio in Sausalito's historic Industrial Center Building (ICB), where she works in both digital and "messy" media. She uses a MacBook Pro and Wacom tablet in live sessions with a nude model, where she specializes in quick gesture drawings. Many of these sketches are then combined into more complex images that are printed on archival papers. Some will inspire work in acrylic, oil, or mixed media collage. Rhoda accepts portrait commissions in both pixels and pigment. Doing business as Rhoda Draws A Crowd, she creates live digital caricature entertainment for trade shows and corporate events. Visit her website at www.rhodadraws.com.

Contents

Acknowledgments

I'm grateful to publisher Stacy Hiquet and everyone at Cengage Learning who made this third edition possible. I want to thank Michelle Arcadipane, Marketing Development Manager and Acquisitions Editor. Thanks to Kezia Endsley, my project and copy editor, for her patience and vigilance. A big hug for Barbara Pollak, who earned her day at the spa for a great technical review. Shawn Morningstar did her usual fantastic layout design. An apology to proofreader Kelly Talbot, because I made so few misteaks (sic). A very special thank you goes to Stewart McKissick, for demonstrating his airbrush cartooning techniques in Lesson 10.

Thanks to all who donated their photos and likenesses to provide source images for the projects: my friends, colleagues, family, and the Pakistani man with the nice smile at the Farmers' Market.

Special thanks go to Jim McCartney and Doug Little at Wacom Technologies, for continuing to raise the bar for pressure-sensitive graphics tablets and for sending me a new tablet every couple of years even though the old ones never break. Intuos4 rules! Finally, I am very grateful to Steve Szoczei at Corel Corporation—kudos to the entire Painter development team for the awesome new features and refinements in Painter 12.

Have Another Layer 39

The Great 'scape 59

Be a People Person 83

Part II Beyond the Basics

9 Fine Art Explorations 163

10 Special Projects............................185

A Fundamentals and Beyond 205

Introduction

Welcome to Corel Painter 12

I'm delighted that Cengage Learning invited me to write this third edition of *Digital Painting Fundamentals with Corel Painter*. The earlier books, for versions X (pronounced "ten") and 11 (pronounced "eleven") were greeted with very positive responses from users and critics, not just my friends and family. This edition has all new projects and I hope many of you are returning for more. The edition for Painter 11 was used by Corel Corporation in several promotions, so I must be doing something right.

This book will get you started using Painter 12. If you are familiar with earlier versions of Painter, it will help you make the transition. You will get a step-by-step instruction for using the basic software and hardware that are the industry standard for pixel-based drawing and painting—Corel Painter and a Wacom graphics tablet. (If you're not sure what a tablet is or what pixels are, see Appendix A, "Fundamentals and Beyond"). Exercises and projects will give you increasing control of tools and techniques. You will acquire and sharpen the skills needed for working in any medium, such as hand-eye coordination and drawing what you see. But there's more to digital art than just knowing how to make a series of marks on an electronic canvas—you will also be introduced to traditional art concepts such as line quality, contrast, and focal point.

With digital art there's no need for the labor of stretching canvas and preparing a surface to accept pigment. You won't need to replenish dried up tubes of paint or replace broken chalks and worn-out brushes. Your clothes won't get spattered with ink, you never need to inhale toxic fumes, and your hands will stay clean. (For artists who would actually miss the messiness of a traditional studio, Wacom might be working on making a leaky pen that smells like turpentine!) You can save every version of a painting as it develops. Your digital paper won't wrinkle, your colors won't fade, and with 32 levels of **Undo** there's no such thing as a mistake. As for storage space, hundreds of drawings and paintings can fit into a few cubic inches of hard drive or on CDs.

A Little History

Unleashed in the early '90s, Painter brought forth a new era for pixel-based digital graphics. Painter was the first "Natural Media Emulation" program, created for artists by artists! With this software, along with the newly developed pressure-sensitive graphics tablets to replace the mouse, artists could now begin to work comfortably at the computer. Painter has matured over the years and remains unrivalled for its capacity to imitate virtually any natural medium. It also has a considerable number of bells and whistles for creating effects that go way beyond what can be produced "naturally."

When Painter was released I was in the right place at the right time (for a change), creating digital caricatures as a booth attraction for Computer Graphics trade shows. I painted with Photoshop then, but when I saw what Painter could do, I knew what my future looked like (how refreshing). I still rely on Photoshop for image manipulation, but Photoshop's brush tool is anemic compared to Painter's robust array of brush styles and controls. Incidentally, these two apps have become more and more compatible over the years. You can create an image in either program, and then open it in the other for additional work, using the best features of each. Taken together, Photoshop and Painter are the dream team for digital painters.

What's New?

Painter 12 has had more than just an interface lift since the previous version—it has undergone major surgery. The **Brush Selector** works in a new and more efficient way, and has been moved to the opposite side of the screen. Icons have been redesigned and there has been a significant reshuffling of **Brush** categories. New features include a robust **Clone Source** panel, **Mirror** and **Kaleidoscope** painting, and a **Real Wet Oil** brush category. A new approach to emulating watercolor techniques, called **Real Watercolor**, provides the most satisfying and convincing solution to watercolor painting yet offered in this program. It's the third one, and both of the previous watercolor categories are still included in the Painter 12 brush library. Customizing Painter has become much easier, including the making of custom icons. I devote a whole lesson in the middle of the book to customizing not only brushes, but also the entire Painter workspace.

Another great new thing happened since the previous version—I changed my name from Rhoda Grossman to Rhoda Draws. It's legal, and I can show you my passport, driver's license, and Nordstrom credit card to prove it.

Who Needs This Book?

If you are in one or more of the following groups, this book is for you.

- Traditional fine artists getting ready to "go digital," or at least willing to give it a try.

- Novice or intermediate users of Corel Painter and Wacom tablets, with little or no art background.

- Photoshop users who want to enhance their creativity with the "other" pixel-based program.

- Health-conscious artists who are literally sick and tired of using toxic materials in their work.

- Hobbyists and digital Sunday painters of all ages, who might need a bit of hand-holding to get started or to go to the next level in their enjoyment of this medium.

- Folks who have played around with drawing on their iPad and want to use more advanced tools.

Others who would be well advised to choose this book as their introduction to Corel Painter are impatient users who don't want to sit through an interminable explanation of every nook and cranny of the program before they're allowed to get their feet wet. In this book you're invited to jump in and splash around almost immediately. If you enjoy the instant gratification of your creative impulses, Painter is just the ticket! When traditional artists get a glimpse of the enormous capabilities of Corel Painter, they can usually overcome any fear of technology that might stand in their way—it happened to me 20 years ago. I was a technophobic artist/illustrator who became suddenly intrigued with digital art in middle-age and managed to create a new career path with my "beginner's mind" and the courage to explore unknown territory. I am now an official tour guide to that territory. I'm still not really a "techie" and that makes me an ideal trainer for people who need a little coaxing to break into digital art. This book will help traditional artists transfer their skills to the computer. It will also show folks who think they have no "talent" that they can learn the basics…then it's just "practice, practice." No prior experience with Painter or other graphics applications is required. Oh, yes—you'll need a Wacom tablet, unless you really prefer drawing with a bar of soap or a hockey puck.

What You Will Learn

Although the word "drawing" doesn't appear in the title of this book, drawing is an essential foundation for painting. Drawing ability, like many skills, is a combination of natural aptitude and training. We don't expect a pianist to simply sit down and play a concerto without years of study and practice, including scales and fingering exercises. Lesson 1, "Welcome to Painter 12," provides exercises to practice eye-hand coordination, control, and technique. Use these exercises for a few minutes before each session to warm up and loosen up before you begin to work. You might never play the piano, but you'll be able to draw one.

Lesson 2, "Draw What You See," introduces basic drawing techniques that you will continue to use throughout the book. If you already have skill using traditional art materials, you'll find it easier to master digital media. If you don't have traditional drawing or painting expertise, you can begin to develop it here. Drawing and painting techniques can be learned and improved by anyone at any age.

The ability to draw is based in large part on the ability to see accurately. You will develop your ability to look critically at your subject, whether it's a still life or a nude model, and observe the shapes, lines, textures, tones, and proportions that are essential to making a successful drawing. The projects presented in these lessons begin with simple assignments and gradually become more challenging. They cover a wide range of subjects and techniques, including:

- Tracing a photo

- Sketching a still life

- Creating a landscape

- Painting a portrait

- Drawing the human figure

- Cloning a photo in different styles

- Abstract painting

- Illustration and graphic techniques

- Experimental animation

- Mixed media painting

Personal fulfillment and More

Sadly, public schools don't offer much to nurture creativity. Art (and, to a lesser extent, music) is neglected and discounted as an esoteric pursuit reserved for the rare person who is "talented" from birth. Most people go through life thinking they have no such "talent", while the truth is they simply haven't learned some basic skills and concepts that can be mastered with practice. Creative expression is not only important for personal fulfillment, but a valuable element in a healthy society.

Appendix A provides some basic terms and definitions, along with other handy bits of information. There are resources for images, fonts, printing, and even a little free legal advice. I also list other books and publications to help you develop as a digital artist. So take a look back there once in a while.

Dude—Where's the CD?

No need to worry where you left the CD with all the source images and other special items to help you work the projects. All of them, and more, are available on a website that supports this book. Go to www.courseptr.com/downloads. You can then search by the book's title, the author's name, or by ISBN to find the correct downloads.

That's where you'll find images and custom palettes needed for the projects, organized by lesson number or by subject categories. There are photos of people, places, and things mostly shot by me, so they are royalty-free. Some of the images were donated by my family and friends. In addition to the specific images I use in each lesson, many more photos are provided for you to choose from or to use in your own projects—just promise to use them for good and not for evil. Corel Painter provides ways to organize your favorite tools and art materials. The **Pals&Libs** folder contains custom palettes and libraries to accompany specific projects, making it easier for you to jump right into a lesson without having to rummage around searching for the recommended brushes, colors, and other items. You'll learn how easy it is to create your own custom palettes and libraries, too.

The **Rhoda Portfolio** folder has samples of my digital art created in successive versions of Painter, spanning nearly 20 years. These show my use of several styles, showcasing the range and versatility of Painter. You'll see some illustration assignments as well as personal projects, portraits, abstract painting, cartooning, and experimental caricature created live at trade shows and other events.

But enough about me. I'll see you in Lesson 1.

This book is not an exhaustive encyclopedia of Painter, so get friendly with the Painter 12 online **Help** feature when you need to know more about a feature or option. I didn't even try to present every aspect of the program, in order to keep the focus on drawing and painting. Our main course is exploring the **Natural Media** brushes, with a few special effects and some image manipulation as side dishes. By the time you finish all the projects in all the lessons, from soup to nuts, you will have digested most Painter techniques and had a nibble of many others. You'll probably find some brushes and tools more to your taste than others. And if you're still hungry for more instruction, there are resources in Appendix A as well as in the Painter 12 **Help** menu.

How to Use This Book

Lessons 1, 2, and 3 (in that order) will give you enough of the fundamentals to get you up and running. After that you can feel free to jump around and do what looks interesting at the moment. Within a lesson it's a good idea to start with the first project and work down, but even that isn't absolutely required. Each lesson begins with a list of images and other items that you need for the projects. Download them to your hard drive in advance and keep them organized in a way that makes sense to you, so you can find them quickly.

Each project is liberally illustrated with images at various stages to keep you on track. Screen captures of dialog boxes, menus, or panels will help you navigate the program and choose options. These screenshots were all made on a Mac, but the difference between them and the Windows version is merely cosmetic. In any case, I'll give keyboard commands for both Mac and PC. For example: **Cmd/Ctrl** means use the **Command** key if you're on a Mac, the **Control** key if you use Windows. Including the keystroke equivalent every time I mention a command will be awkward, so I included a list of the most popular keyboard shortcuts in Appendix A. A much more inclusive list is provided in Painter 12, under **Preferences > Customize Keys**.

Corel has brought significant changes to Painter in this version, but users of previous versions have not been ignored in this book. You'll be given tips along the way, pointing out new features that are available only in Painter 12, and a mention of how some options are implemented in earlier versions. Photoshop users will find a great many Painter tools, palettes, and commands are the same or similar to what they are accustomed to.

The Basics

1 Welcome to Painter 12

I made these scribbles with several of the brush variants available in Painter 12. In just a few minutes, you'll actually be able to create digital scribbles as good as this! So, turn on your computer, plug in your Wacom tablet, launch your Painter program, and let's get started.

For this lesson, you'll use the following item from the website that supports this book:

- Custom palette: **Painter 12 Sampler**

When you see the Welcome screen, shown in Figure 1.1, you can choose **Create a New Image**, but first notice some other options. **Brush Tracking,** under the **Set-up** section, is an essential feature for adjusting your Wacom tablet to your touch. Click it now to get the panel shown in Figure 1.2. Make a typical stroke in the blank rectangle. The colorful squiggle gives Painter the pressure and speed data it needs to optimize the tablet for you. You can access **Brush Tracking** at any time in Painter's **Preferences**.

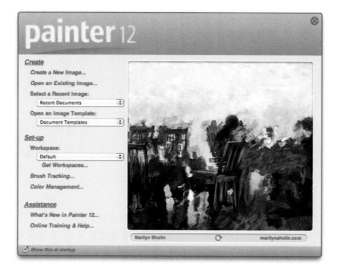

Figure 1.1

You're welcome.

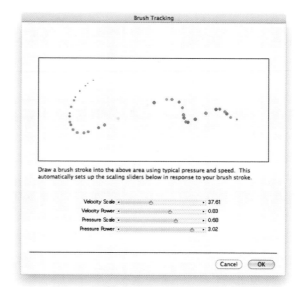

Figure 1.2

One good squiggle.

Okay, now you're ready to create that new image. The **New Image** dialog box, shown in Figure 1.3, lets you enter height, width, and resolution for the image. In this book, you'll use 72 ppi (pixels per inch) most of the time, so you'll be able to see the whole Painter Canvas onscreen without scrolling and work faster. (Pixels and resolution are explained in Appendix A.) Canvas color is white unless you click the color swatch to change it. **Basic Paper** is the default surface texture, but that tiny triangle in the lower-right corner of the paper swatch lets you choose from several alternatives. If you want to use the same settings over again, click the plus sign and you'll be able to save the current configuration as a new preset.

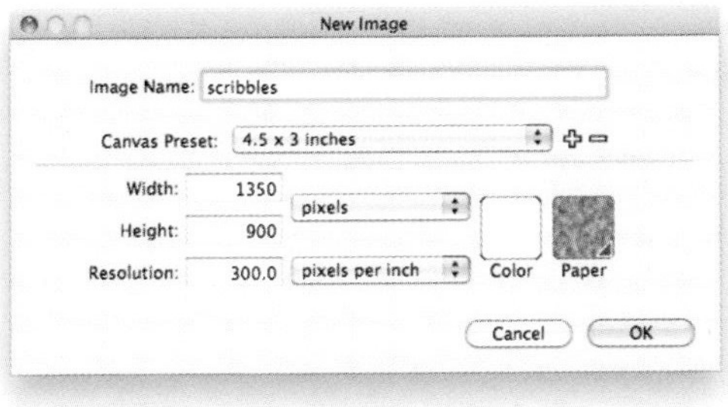

Figure 1.3
Choose size, resolution, color, and texture.

Getting Acquainted with Painter

In addition to your canvas, the Painter workspace consists of several panels offering brushes and other art supplies as well as special features and commands. All panels are listed in the **Window** menu. You'll see the vertical **Toolbox** on the left side of your screen. I used Painter's **Preferences > Interface** to make the single column of tools into a double column. Make sure the **Brush** tool is selected, as shown in Figure 1.4. A tool or option is blue when active. If all you want to do is draw and paint, you can ignore most of the other choices in the **Toolbox** for quite a while.

So Many Choices

If you're new to Painter, the sheer number of options, palettes, tools, and menus can seem overwhelming. There are ways to control the clutter and tell Painter how you like to work. I'll introduce you to workspace management as you go, but it might take a while before you know what some of your preferences are.

When working with Painter you will have only one actual tool in your hand—the Wacom pen. Hold it as shown in Figure 1.5. Avoid touching the lever on the side of the pen's barrel. (It has click functions that won't be useful while you're drawing.) This model is the medium-sized Intuos 4. Pressure sensitivity enables you to control the width and/or opacity of your stroke by varying how hard you press the tip of the pen to the tablet as you work. Many of Painter's natural media brushes also respond to the tilt of your Wacom pen.

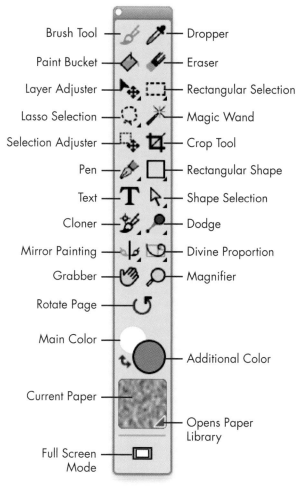

Brush Tool — Dropper
Paint Bucket — Eraser
Layer Adjuster — Rectangular Selection
Lasso Selection — Magic Wand
Selection Adjuster — Crop Tool
Pen — Rectangular Shape
Text — Shape Selection
Cloner — Dodge
Mirror Painting — Divine Proportion
Grabber — Magnifier
Rotate Page
Main Color
— Additional Color
Current Paper
— Opens Paper Library
Full Screen Mode

Figure 1.4
The Brush tool is good to go.

Figure 1.5
Jewelry sold separately.

The marks you make with your Wacom pen and Painter can imitate virtually any traditional art materials. You'll choose your digital "brush" with the **Brush Selector** in the upper-left corner of the Painter workspace. It has two main sections, one for the colorful icons representing each of 29 categories and the other for the specific variant within the selected category. Below them is the **Dab and Stroke Preview**, showing a cross-section of the brush tip and a sample stroke made with black. Figure 1.6 shows that the **Wet Brush** variant of the **Acrylics** category is the current choice. Notice that the **Wet Brush** variant runs out of pigment rather quickly. What the **Dab and Stroke Preview** cannot show is how this brush behaves when strokes are overlapped. Figure 1.7 shows several **Wet Brush** strokes made with different colors. This brush also acts like a brush in the **Blender** category, smearing colors together. Go ahead, give it a try.

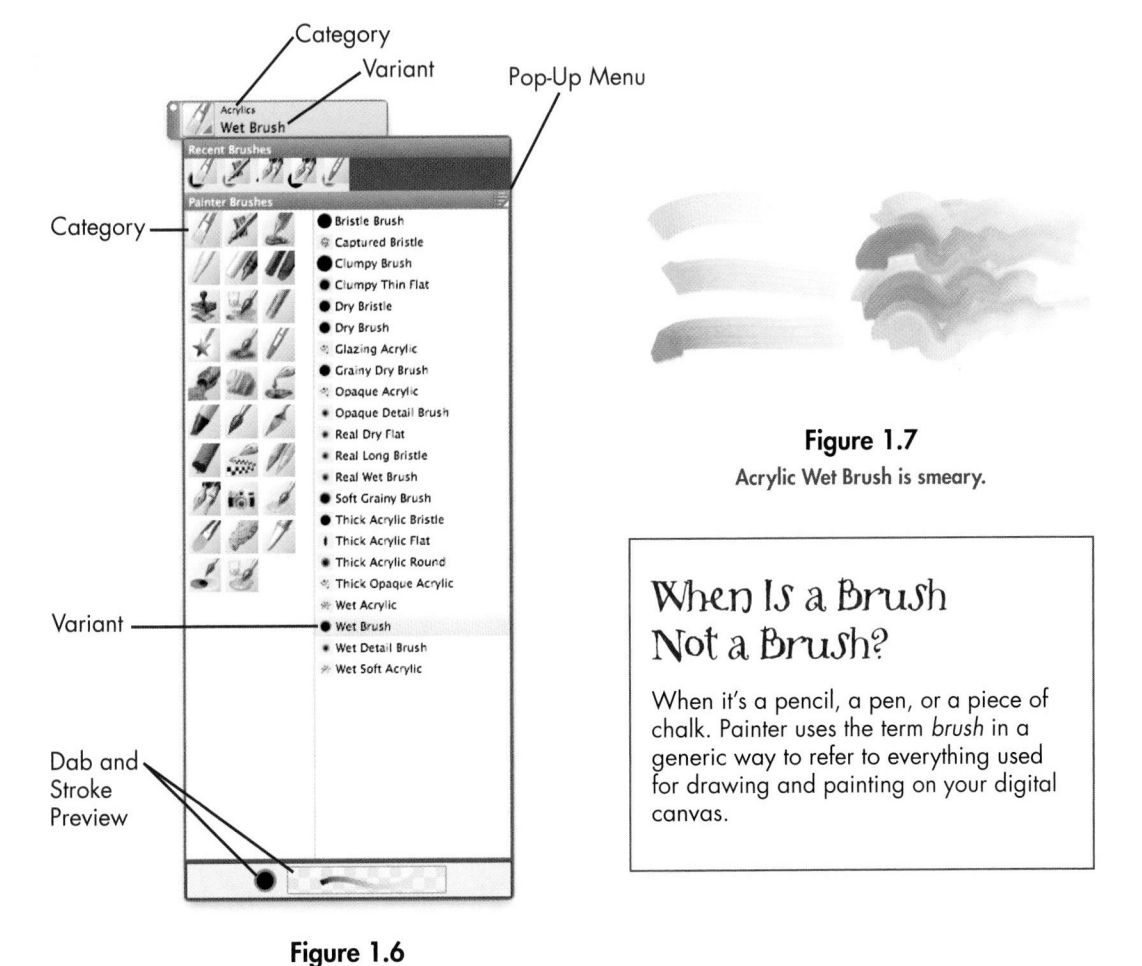

Figure 1.7

Acrylic Wet Brush is smeary.

When Is a Brush Not a Brush?

When it's a pencil, a pen, or a piece of chalk. Painter uses the term *brush* in a generic way to refer to everything used for drawing and painting on your digital canvas.

Figure 1.6

The Brush Selector shows the current category and variant.

You can change the color of pigment using the **Color** panel shown in Figure 1.8. Click anywhere on the **Hue** ring to choose a position on the color wheel, and then click inside the triangle for the exact **Value** (brightness) and **Saturation** (purity) you want. There are other panels for creating new colors and grouping them. See Appendix A for more info on managing color.

Until you get familiar with what each category icon represents, you might find it helpful to see the names of the categories alongside a smaller icon. Use the pop-up menu in the upper-right corner of the **Brush Selector** to choose the list view from **Category Display**. This menu has several other options, such as hiding the **Dab and Stroke Preview**. Figure 1.9 shows the categories as a list, with **Dab and Stroke Preview** and **Recent Brushes** gone.

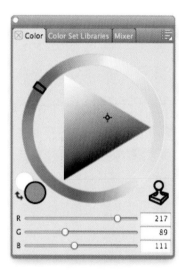

Figure 1.8
Pick a color, any color.

Figure 1.9
Categories and variants listed.

Department of Redundancy Department

It's handy to be able to click on a brush you used a few minutes ago without having to search for it again in these long lists, but **Recent Brushes** also appear in the **Property Bar** at the top of your screen. The **Property Bar** shown in Figure 1.10 shows the default settings for a **Pastel** variant, along with several other handy choices that are useful when drawing and painting. The **Property Bar** shows options for whatever item in the **Toolbox** is active.

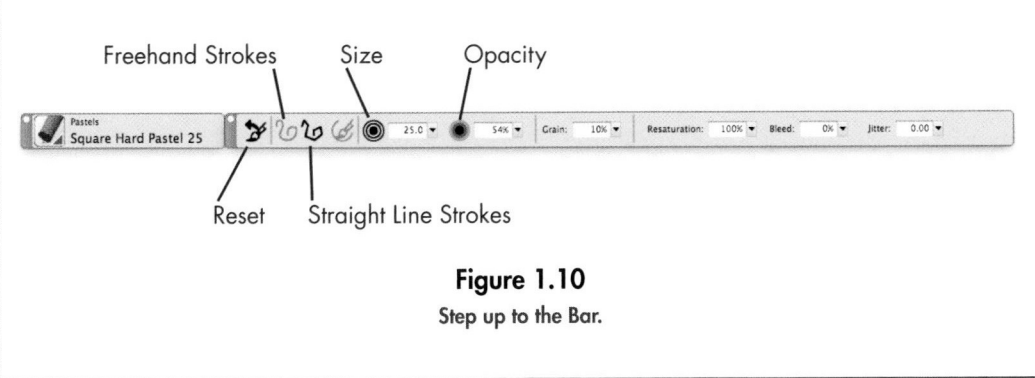

Freehand Strokes   Size   Opacity

Reset   Straight Line Strokes

Figure 1.10
Step up to the Bar.

Let's Doodle

Now that you've got your canvas (and your feet) wet, switch to a few other categories and scribble a bit. You'll try out some **Pencils, Markers,** and **Pastels** (pastels are like chalk, only softer and much more expensive). Choose **Square Hard Pastel** from the **Pastels** category. A close-up of the **Dab and Stroke Preview** is shown in Figure 1.11 along with the actual dab or footprint of the brush and two strokes. The strokes were made with different paper textures, showing how well this variant imitates the response to paper grain of traditional pastel sticks.

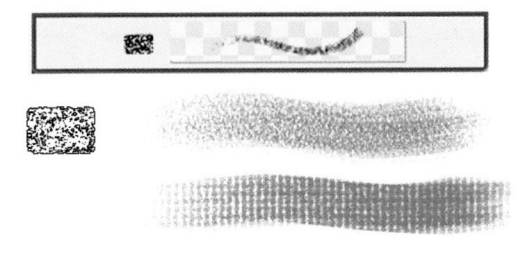

Figure 1.11
Have a Dab and a Stroke.

Brush Ghosting

As your Wacom pen hovers over the canvas, you may want to see the "ghost" of the dab between strokes. There are a few other choices for the cursor, available in the **Preferences > Interface** panel shown in Figure 1.12. **Enhanced Brush Ghost** shows you the angle of your Wacom pen (as if you couldn't tell) and can result in performance lags for some brushes.

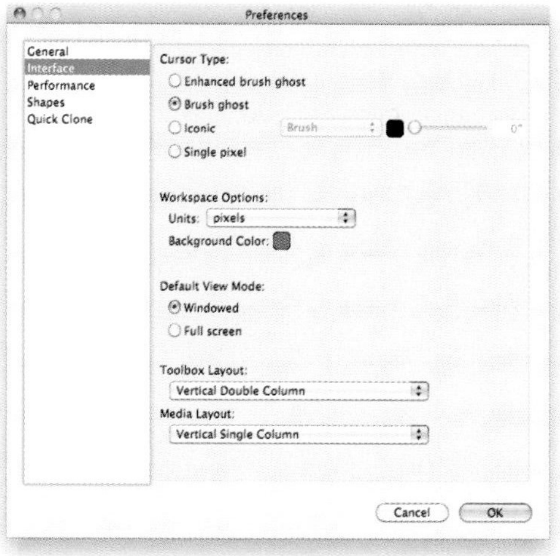

Figure 1.12

Interface preferences.

The three small rectangles in Figure 1.13 show the colors I used to make additional strokes with **Square Hard Pastel,** then **Thick n Thin Marker,** and finally the **Real 6B Soft Pencil.** You might expect pastels and chalk to reveal the surface texture of the paper and digital dry media does not disappoint. Lighter pressure reveals more of the paper surface because heavy strokes tend to fill in the depressions. Painter uses the term *grainy* for this behavior. Chalk and pastels are opaque, so light colors can cover darker ones. By contrast, overlapping marker strokes build up, getting darker and denser. Painter uses the terms *cover* and *buildup* to describe these two basic methods for determining the behavior of a brush variant.

Square Hard Pastel

Thick n Thin Marker

Real 6B Soft Pencil

Figure 1.13

Pencils and markers and chalk, oh my!

I Love the Pressure!

Make some strokes and squiggles with each of these variants, changing the pressure and speed of your pen. Did your strokes respond to pressure variations? Even more important, did the lines appear where you wanted them? Use the "Test Your Tablet" tip to confirm that your Wacom tablet is functioning properly. If pen strokes require more pressure than you're comfortable with, or (on the other hand) if the pen seems too sensitive to pressure changes, recall that you can customize the tablet's sensitivity within Painter by using **Preferences > Brush Tracking**.

To change from the default **Basic Paper** to a different type of surface, open the **Paper Library** near the bottom of the **Toolbox**, or choose the **Papers** panel from the **Windows** menu. Figure 1.14 shows the **Papers** panel with the current library of swatches. There are sliders to change size and other qualities of the paper grain.

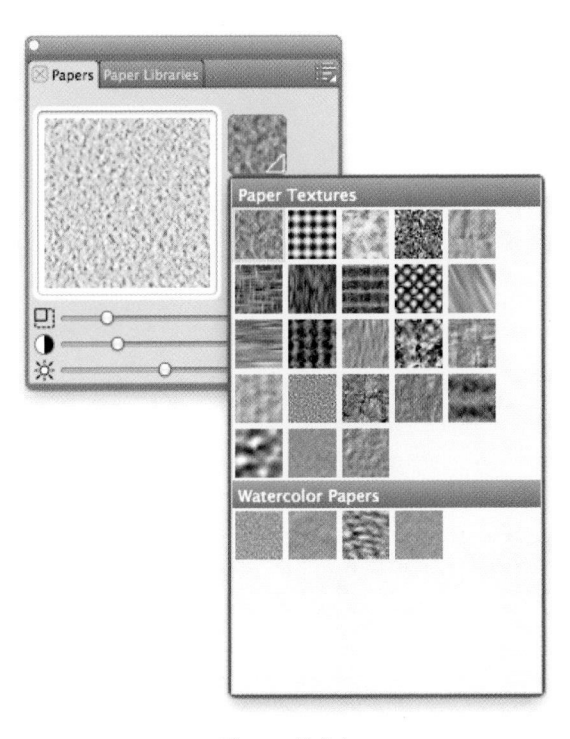

Test Your Tablet

Make sure the tablet is mapped to your computer screen by doing the "two-point test." Touch the point of your pen to any corner of the active area of the tablet and notice that your cursor shows up at the corresponding corner of your screen. That was one point. (If that didn't work, you're in trouble—see the Wacom tablet section in Appendix A.) Now lift the pen away from the tablet (don't drag it!) and touch it to the opposite/diagonal corner. If the cursor shows up in the new position, you're good to go. If not, see Appendix A.

Figure 1.14
Papers, please!

Get Real

Have you tried the **Real 6B Soft Pencil** yet? Look once again at the strokes in the bottom row of Figure 1.13. Marks made with the Wacom pen held upright are thin lines, but as you tilt your pen the lines become wider. It's possible to make a very wide stroke if you change your grip so that the pen is at a steep angle. This imitates sketching and shading with the side of a pencil or pigment stick. For a photo of this grip see Figure 3.3 in Lesson 3, "Have Another Layer," where you'll use this technique in an illustration project.

Traditional paintbrushes can have a variety of shapes and are composed of numerous bristles that can range in length, thickness, and stiffness. The kind of mark made by a bristle brush depends on a large number of factors: quality and number of bristles, viscosity and amount of paint loaded, and the pressure and direction of the artist's stroke. There are several Painter categories devoted to bristle-type brushes. They include **Acrylics, Oils, and Impasto** (Italian for *thick paint*). Take a couple of variants from each of these categories for a test drive. As you did with the **Acrylics Wet Brush** earlier, notice how strokes interact with each other. The following variants made the dabs and strokes shown in Figure 1.15.

> **Acrylic: Clumpy Brush**
>
> **Oils: Fine Camel**
>
> **Impasto: Smeary Bristle Spray**

The green and pink dabs made with the **Acrylic Clumpy Brush** are squeezed ovals, like plump grains of rice. There is a slight variation in the size and brightness of bristles. Short strokes have ragged edges at the beginning and end. Longer strokes fade out gradually, losing color but continuing to show bristle striations.

Figure 1.15
Different strokes.

The footprint of **Fine Camel Oils** looks like a spray of tiny bristles. Use a light touch for a smooth opaque stroke. Increased pressure makes the bristles spread out, showing spaces between them. It's hard to see the delicate dab of **Smeary Bristle Spray** from the **Impasto** category. Like the **Fine Camel Oil**, strokes show spaces between bristles. But this brush, as its name suggests, picks up underlying color and smears it. The impasto effect can be turned off in the **Navigator** settings shown in Figure 1.16.

Open Navigator Settings

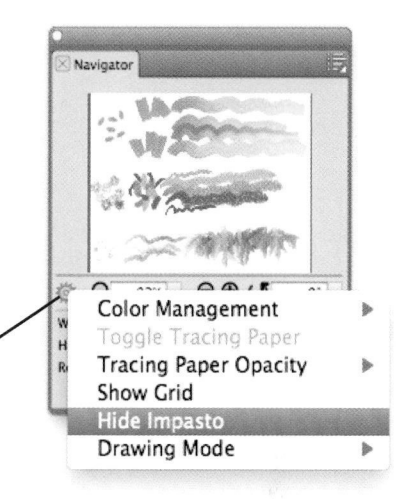

Figure 1.16

Navigator settings.

So Many Choices!

Every new version of Painter introduces one or more exciting new categories, and Painter 12 unveils **Real Watercolor** and **Real Wet Oil**. To keep the sheer number of categories under control, some of them have been combined. For example, **Pastels** and **Oil Pastels** are now grouped together in **Pastels**. Several other categories and variants have been reshuffled. Painter 11 users will get used to the new system quickly, but there is also the option of loading the "legacy" Painter 11 brushes. The pop-up menu in the **Brush Selector** offers the choice of **Brush Library**.

Any way you slice and dice the categories, there are nearly a thousand variants to choose from! Just exploring a fraction of them and keeping track of the ones you like can be a challenge. Fortunately, there are ways to organize brushes and quickly find the ones you need for a project.

Custom Palettes

After you've been working with Painter for a while you'll probably have some favorite brushes and paper textures. They can be collected in a compact little palette that can be used over and over. *Custom palettes* are easy to make. Choose a brush variant you want, and press the **Shift** key while you drag the brush icon away from the **Brush Selector**. A new custom palette is created containing that brush. Add more brushes by simply dragging in more items. Hold the Shift key down to remove or reposition items. Figure 1.17 shows the first two items in a custom palette, a **Pastel** variant and a **Blender**. There are custom palettes provided for many of the projects in the following lessons. They can be downloaded to your hard drive from the website that supports this book (see www.courseptr.com/downloads).

Figure 1.17
Shift and drag.

Meanwhile, Back at the Palettes

You can create a different custom palette for sketching, painting, working with photos, or for any specific project. Manage them with the **Custom Palette Organizer,** shown in Figure 1.18, by choosing **Window > Custom Palette > Organizer**. Give them descriptive names and save them using the **Export** command. Load them with the **Import** command.

Custom Palette Organizer
Custom Palette

Painter 12 sampler
Custom 3

Rename...
Delete

Import...
Export...

Done

Figure 1.18
Get organized.

Back to the Drawing Board

Your first assignment is to fill a blank canvas with scribbles and strokes, using the twelve brushes in a custom palette shown in Figure 1.19. Download this **Painter 12 Sampler** palette from the website that supports this book. Or just make it from scratch, using the following list. Brushes are in alphabetical order by category, starting at the upper left of the palette.

Top row:

- Acrylics > Real Wet Brush
- Airbrushes > Pixel Spray
- Artists > Impressionist
- Blenders > Water Rake

Middle row:

- Charcoal & Conte > Real Hard Conte
- Impasto > Gloopy
- Oils > Flat Oils
- Palette Knives > Dry Palette Knife

Bottom row:

- Pastels > Square Hard Pastel
- Pencils > Grainy Pencil
- Pens > Dry Ink
- Digital Watercolor > Broad Water Brush

Figure 1.19
The brush sampler.

Scribble a Sampler

Just because your main purpose is to get familiar with brushes, that doesn't mean your work can't look good. To help make something more pleasing to the eye, restrict yourself to one color or family of colors. A limited color palette tends to create visual harmony even with lots of variety in brush strokes, texture, and detail. You may change the saturation and brightness of the main color by clicking in the triangle of the **Color** panel, but stick with the same position on the **Hue** ring. Consider grouping your scribbles to make a composition based on shapes or other variables. My sampler, shown in Figure 1.20, is based on three horizontal strips. Each one uses only the variants for the corresponding row in the custom palette. By the time I got to the third row, I started to get the hang of it.

Figure 1.20
The scribbler.

Let's examine some of the brushes in the sampler palette more closely. The **Impressionist** variant is composed of a narrow spray of tear-drop shaped dabs, which follow the direction of your stroke. Increased pressure makes the dabs darker and larger. Overlapping **Impressionist** strokes can make for very painterly effects. Like the other variants in the **Artists** category, the **Impressionist** brush is designed to imitate important techniques from art history. The **Seurat** brush is named after the French painter who invented the technique of pointillism, where tiny dots of color combine optically for the viewer. This brush sprays overlapping dots of variable hue and value (brightness). The **Van Gogh** variant also has built-in color variability. Each stroke is composed of several thick bristles differing slightly in hue and more strongly in value. There is a random quality between strokes—no two strokes are exactly alike. This brush is most effective when short strokes are applied in different directions. The **Sargent** brush, a tribute to the portrait painter John Singer Sargent, has no color variation but does have a smeary quality that contributes to its creamy, luscious look. Figure 1.21 demonstrates all four of these special variants.

Gloopy is a very thick **Impasto** stroke, and usually takes several seconds to be fully formed. A short stroke is best unless you have a few errands to run. One of my favorite brushes is **Dry Ink**, now included among the **Pens**, but previously in the **Calligraphy** category and somewhere else before that. (Every time there is a new version of Painter, I have to go hunting for it.) **Dry Ink** is an opaque, juicy, and bristly brush, with a very wide range of thickness based on pressure. The **Broad Water** brush successfully imitates the translucency of watercolor, as well as the wet fringe effect (pooling of pigment at the edges of a stroke).

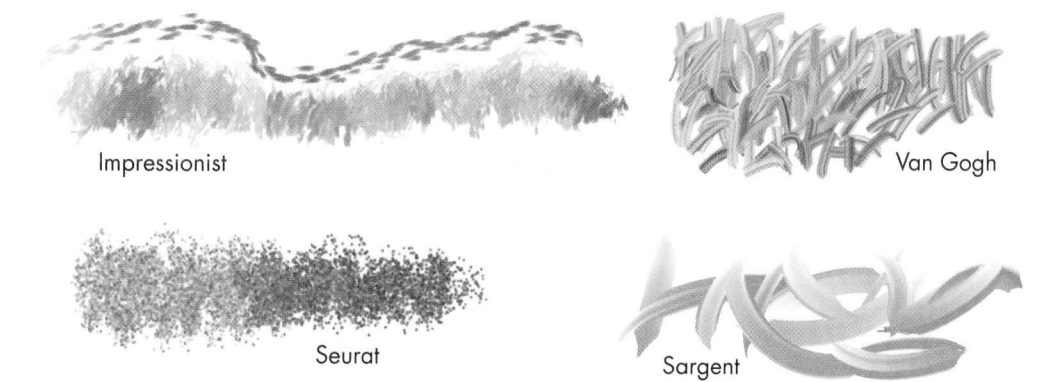

Impressionist

Van Gogh

Seurat

Sargent

Figure 1.21
Famous artists.

Proceed at Your Own Risk!

Explore other brush categories now, or any time, but be warned—some of them are exotic, to say the least. For example, **Pattern** pens don't apply the current color, but paint with the current pattern (you'll find that library right under **Papers** at the bottom of the **Toolbox**). **Watercolor** and **Real Watercolor** brushes require a special layer, created automatically when you use them. **Liquid Ink** is in a class (and layer) by itself. As for the **Image Hose**—don't get me started!

Control Yourself

Here are some exercises for developing skill with the Wacom tablet. Use them as a warm-up before you begin a session, and to check whether you need to reset the **Brush Tracker** for your pressure and speed. Do the exercises in the order given. If you save your practice canvases, you can observe your progress from one session to another.

Crosshatching

Start with a new white canvas about 6 inches square at 72 ppi. Choose **Pen > Ball Point Pen** and use black as the main color. Refer to Figure 1.22 as you work. Make a long mark at the angle natural for you. I'm right-handed, so my strokes will slant slightly to the left. There is

Figure 1.22
Hatch and crosshatch.

no width variation in this pen, just like its real-world counterpart. If you need too much pressure to get a strong line, use a light touch. Your second stroke should be parallel to the first and reasonably close to it. Add several more strokes the same distance apart. Go for accuracy the first few times, and then increase your speed.

Next, use the **Rotate Page** tool and make another series of lines at right angles to the first set. After that, tilt the page so you can add lines at a 45 degree angle. You can probably guess the next step. Crosshatching skill comes in handy when you want to develop shading and volume in drawings.

Pressure Practice

Make a new canvas for the next exercise or simply clear this one, using **Select All (Cmd/Ctrl+A)** followed by **Delete/Backspace.** Switch to the **Dry Ink** brush, which was used in your sampler painting. This is the ideal variant for practicing pressure control. Make a long stroke that begins with very light pen pressure and gradually increase pressure to the maximum width, then taper off as you end the stroke. It might take several tries to get the right touch for a smooth transition. Check out the practice strokes in Figure 1.23, some of which are more successful than others.

Sensitivity Training

Making smooth transitions in line width will be easier if you are using a Wacom tablet with greater pressure sensitivity. The Intuos 4 models have 2,048 levels, and **Bamboo Fun** has 1,024 levels. The entry-level **Bamboo** pen has "only" 512 levels. Fewer levels of pressure makes it even more important to tweak the settings in **Preferences > Brush Tracking.**

Figure 1.23
Ink under pressure.

What's Next?

You're off to a good start. You have a basic understanding of how to choose and organize Painter brushes and how to show your Wacom tablet who's boss. In the following lessons, you'll practice skills and learn concepts for improving your mastery of drawing and painting. I promise to take you way beyond scribbling!

2 Draw What You See

You'll begin with a relatively simple subject and practice drawing it using several methods. First, you'll draw the outline. Then you'll add shading and color. Each new technique will teach you more about how to draw and how to use Painter 12.

For this lesson, you'll use the following items from the website that supports this book:

- Images: **delicious3.jpg** and **apples_bowl.jpg**
- Custom palettes: **Basic drawing palette**

An Apple a Day

One of the best assignments I ever had in a traditional art class was to create a series of 20 versions of an apple, each using a different medium or style. There are several photos of apples in the **Things > Food** folder on the website that supports this book. They all look good enough to eat, and draw (not necessarily in that order). Open **delicious3.jpg,** shown in Figure 2.1.

Figure 2.1
It's a delicious.

Size Matters

You may want to change the size of the apple image to fit your screen. That's easy. **Canvas > Resize** brings up the dialog box shown in Figure 2.2. Before you enter the new height or width, be sure to uncheck **Constrain File Size**. If you don't, the change in dimensions will be compensated with a change in resolution, and the image will be exactly the same size onscreen!

Figure 2.2
Your file size may vary.

Clone-and-Trace

Take a look at the edges of the apple shape. It is made up of a series of curves. The easiest way to draw the outline of this shape is to trace it, and the way to set up Painter's tracing function is **File > Quick Clone**. With the **Quick Clone** command, Painter automatically creates an exact copy of the image, names it **Clone of delicious3.jpg**, and deletes the image to give you a blank canvas. You will see a "ghost" of the original apple, however, because the **Tracing Paper** feature is on. Toggle **Tracing Paper** on and off (**Cmd/Ctrl+T**) as the drawing or painting develops. The original image will stay open only if you chose that option in the **Quick Clone** section of **Painter Preferences**. Figure 2.3 shows the **Clone Source** panel, with a tiny thumbnail image of the apple.

Opacity Capacity

Painter X (pronounced "ten") introduced changeable opacity for tracing paper. In Painter 12 (pronounced "twelve"), the tracing paper controls are found in **Navigator Settings** and also in the new **Clone Source** panel. The percentage indicates the hiding power, so the higher the value, the more opaque the tracing paper and the less you can see the original image. This is a handy feature for accommodating different stages in your drawing or different kinds of source images.

Figure 2.3

Delicious apple source.

Use **Window > Custom Palette > Organizer** to import **BasicDrawing.PAL**, shown in Figure 2.4. When your stylus hovers over an item in a custom palette, the icon shows in full color and a "tooltip" gives you the name of the variant.

Pick a dark reddish brown as your primary color and choose **Flattened Pencil** from the custom palette. You're ready to trace. Ignore the cast shadow for now, but do include the stem and a bit of the curve to indicate the depression where the stem emerges. This pencil variant doesn't have much thick-to-thin variation when you apply pressure, so I overlapped a couple of strokes to emphasize weight at the bottom of the shape. Figure 2.5 shows my effort. Don't forget to turn off **Tracing Paper** to see your drawing!

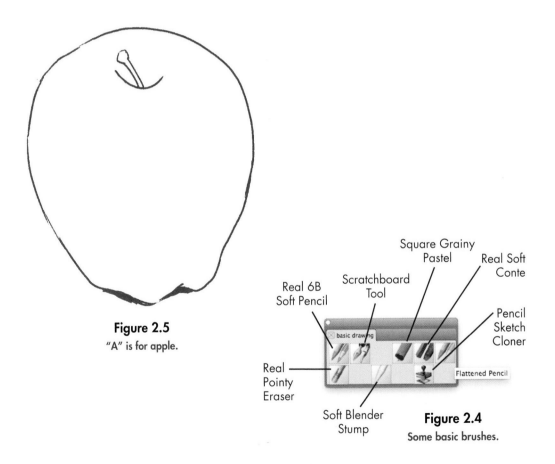

Figure 2.5
"A" is for apple.

Figure 2.4
Some basic brushes.

Dude! Where's My Clone Source? NEW 12

Painter 12 introduces a powerful new way to organize your source images for tracing and cloning. Use the **Clone Source** panel to designate any open image as the one you want, or click the **Open Source Image** icon to browse for any other image on your computer. Be sure to save your work in **Painter's RIFF** format to preserve the **Clone Source** info, even after you close the file. Without an image as the clone source, all versions of Painter default to the current pattern.

Tonal Drawing

The outline drawing looks flat, of course. Open the apple photo again, if you need to, and notice the areas of light and shadow. You'll do another drawing that emphasizes these light and dark variations, so you can create the illusion of depth. A traditional way to render light and dark involves working on medium gray or tinted paper. Paper color does a lot of the work, and all you have to do is add the lightest and darkest parts.

With the **Dropper** tool, sample a medium red or pink color near the bright highlights on the photo. Use **File > Quick Clone** for a fresh canvas. Choose **Set Paper Color** from the **Canvas** menu. Nothing happened yet, but when you **Select > All (Cmd/Ctrl+A)** followed by **Delete/Backspace**, your new rosy color will fill the blank canvas.

Here's What Happened

Painter defines **Paper Color** as whatever an eraser reveals. When you select a new current color, and then choose **Set Paper Color** followed by the select-and-delete maneuver, you have in effect erased the entire canvas, revealing the new color.

This time use a **Conte** stick for the dark outline, and then switch to white for the left edge, indicating the light source. Traditional French Conte sticks are firmer and creamier than chalk or charcoal, and **Painter** emulates them rather well. As with any new brush variant, make a few test strokes and scribble on a "scratch pad" canvas. Adjust the pressure sensitivity of your tablet if needed, using **Painter's Preferences > Brush Tracking**. Figure 2.6 was done with **Real Soft Conte,** reduced in size to about 12 pixels. Notice that there are a couple of breaks in the outline. This is deliberate, allowing some ambiguity between the foreground shape and the background.

Now that you have the outline, you don't really need **Tracing Paper** anymore, so turn it off and use the "eyeball" method—just look at the source photo to guide your placement of highlights and shadows. (This is a good reason to keep the source image open!) Apply a few white strokes in the light areas, pressing harder in the brightest spots. Use dark brown to create some shadow areas. Switch between white and brown as you work by sampling with the **Dropper**.

Don't let light and dark strokes overlap or even touch each other, but rely on the paper color to express mid-tones. Only a few strokes are needed to bring out this form. Refer to Figure 2.6 for guidance and encouragement. White strokes on the highlight areas help to suggest volume. Adding the cast shadow places the apple in a three-dimensional space, as does the addition of more white behind the left side of the shape.

Toggle Your Dropper

A speedy way to sample colors is to hold down the **Option/Alt** key. This changes your brush to the **Dropper** so you can tap your stylus on any desired color in your image. Release the modifier key and your brush tool is back.

Figure 2.6
A hint of depth.

Crosshatch Contours

Take another close look at the apple photo. This time, concentrate on its rounded contours. You'll work on white paper with black lines. Tone and form will be built up from overlapping strokes that follow the contours of the fruit. This hatching and crosshatching is another traditional method, often used by cartoonists and graphic artists, especially for commercial black-and-white printing.

Make another **Quick Clone** of the photo. Choose the **Scratchboard Tool** pen from the **Basic Drawing** custom palette. Changes in pressure will affect the thickness of the lines, so take a few minutes to practice line control. Tweak the sensitivity of your tablet again, if needed. Figure 2.7 has some practice crosshatching made with the **Scratchboard Tool**.

A Real Page Turner

To keep from twisting your wrist too much, use Painter's **Rotate Page** tool, available in all versions. It's the very last item in the **Toolbox**. When you're ready to return to normal orientation, double-click the **Rotate Page** tool.

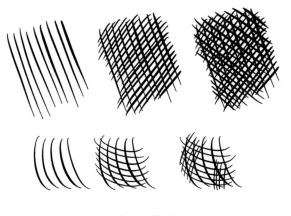

Figure 2.7
Scratch and hatch.

Sketch the stem and outer edges of the apple quickly, and begin to make a series of roughly parallel strokes that follow the curves of the fruit. Use strokes that vary in length and spacing as you build up the form. For darker areas, overlap strokes in different directions. Refer to Figure 2.8 as you go.

Figure 2.8
Fruity buildup.

Clone College

You've been using the tracing feature available with cloning, but Painter's cloning features are capable of so much more! With **Cloner** brushes you can turn photos into drawings or paintings in *virtually* any style, not by clicking on global filter effects, but creating them one brush stroke at a time.

Another Bite at the Apple

Make a fresh **Quick Clone** of the apple photo. Choose the **Cloner** brush in the custom palette (it looks like a rubber stamp). This particular Cloner variant is the **Pencil Sketch Cloner**. Don't choose black this time, or any color at all, because **Cloner** brushes automatically get all color data (hue, saturation, and brightness) from the source image! A glance at the **Color** panel shown in Figure 2.9 confirms that color choices are grayed out and unavailable.

Use some crosshatching techniques once again, along with "controlled scribbling" to build up the form. Concentrate on a couple of focal points, such as the stem area, the highlight, or the bumps at the bottom. This very sketchy style works best when you leave quite a bit of paper showing, as in Figure 2.10.

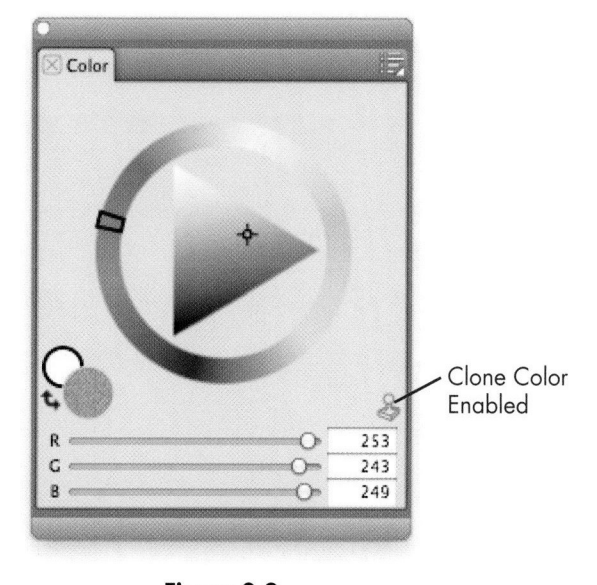

Figure 2.9
Color comes from the source image.

Figure 2.10
Kinda sketchy.

Starter Still Life

For a bit more variety, open **apples_bowl.jpeg**, shown in Figure 2.11. It's a basic still life with lots of colors and a full range of tonality from bright white to dense black. You could use a bit more space at the left of the image, where the bowl touches the edge, so add some pixels where needed. Use **Canvas > Canvas Size**, adding 50 pixels on the left.

Figure 2.11
Two Macs and a Jonathan.

Make a **Quick Clone** of the source photo. Use **Pencil Sketch Cloner** to sketch a rough outline of the apples and the bowl, as shown in Figure 2.12. **Tracing Paper** is at 70%, so you can see more of the drawing and less of the photo.

Find the **Chalk Cloner** in the list of variants for the **Cloner** category. The default size of this brush is 9 pixels, as you can see in the **Property Bar**. Double that to 18 pixels by moving the size slider to the right. Figure 2.13 shows that action. If you want to return the brush to its default size later, you don't have to remember that it was 9 pixels; just click the **Reset Tool** icon in the **Property Bar**.

Figure 2.12
Cloned outlines.

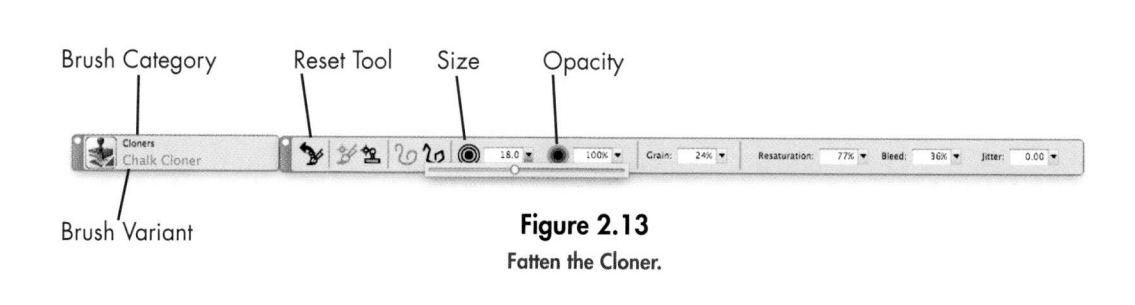

Figure 2.13
Fatten the Cloner.

A fatter **Chalk Cloner** will give less detail in each stroke, so you can rough the colors in quickly. You will pick out some areas to accent later with the original 9-pixels size. **Tracing Paper** can be toggled off at this point, because the pencil sketch outlines will serve as your guide, while you observe the original photo beside it. Using what you learned a few pages ago about following contours with your brush strokes, take the painting to the next stage with your chubby chalk, as shown in Figure 2.14. Not having to decide color or value can give you such freedom!

Continue to develop the volumes with some crosshatch strokes. Allow a few bits of white to show through. The version in Figure 2.15 has slightly more detail for the three stems, made with the original 9-pixel **Chalk Cloner**. This is a lively, energetic drawing. Or is it a painting?

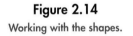

Figure 2.14
Working with the shapes.

Figure 2.15
Juicy fruit!

Drawing or Painting?

What's the difference? Sometimes not much, and I sometimes use these terms interchangeably. In general, drawings are made with dry media, and paintings with wet. Or, if you render your subject mostly with lines, it's a drawing. But when tones and colors blend into each other without distinct edges, it's a painting. A traditional term for artwork composed with a variety of wet and dry materials, possibly incorporating photos or collage elements pasted on, is "mixed media." Technically, everything you make in Painter is "painting" because it's done with pixels. Digital "drawing" requires a vector-based program like Illustrator. I'm glad I could clear that up.

Clone with Style

Artists who work with traditional chalk or pastels generally choose special tinted paper. You'll learn to do that for the next version, and also choose the surface texture of the paper. But first, let's alter the colors of the source image.

Open the **Underpainting** panel shown in Figure 2.16. You'll find it in a group of **Auto-Painting** panels, which have nothing to do with your car. Several intuitive ways to adjust the colors in a photo are provided. The **Color Scheme** and **Photo Enhance** presets can be chosen based on the style of clone painting you prefer. Pick the **Color Scheme** optimized for chalk drawing. The image detail shown in Figure 2.17 has less saturated, warmer colors.

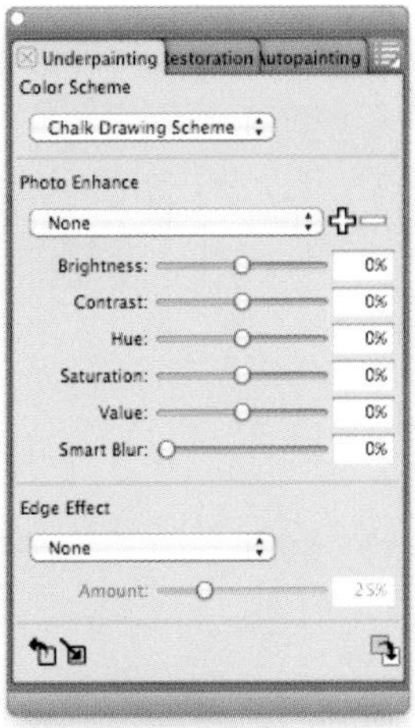

Figure 2.16
The Underpainting panel.

Figure 2.17
Warmed-up apples.

Make a fresh **Quick Clone** of the apples in a bowl. Sample a warm light brown from the wooden planks or just choose a pleasing neutral color for the paper. Use the technique for changing paper color you did earlier, or just "pour" the new color into the clone with the **Paint Bucket**. It won't matter unless you erase. My motto, incidentally is "Life is short—don't erase." I actually had this printed on 500 golf pencils.

Make a Cloner

You can turn a variant from any category into a **Cloner** brush instantly. All you do is click the little rubber stamp icon in the **Color** panel. The hue ring and value/saturation triangle will go gray, indicating that your brush is now using **Clone Color**. You can toggle regular color control back on by clicking the **Rubber Stamp** icon again.

Instead of working with the **Chalk Cloner** this time, turn **Square Hard Pastel** from the custom palette into a **Cloner**, by enabling **Clone Color**. Increase its size to about 25 pixels. A **Hard Pastel** shows paper grain very boldly, so it's important to choose a paper that will enhance the painting. Figure 2.18 shows three possible textures that are available in the **Paper** library. From left to right, they are **Italian Watercolor**, **Coarse Cotton Canvas,** and **Pebble Board**. You can adjust the size of the paper grain, as well as its strength, by changing the brightness and/or contrast of the paper element. Open the **Papers** panel, shown in Figure 2.19, to make those changes as desired.

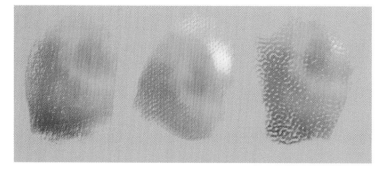

Figure 2.18

Papers, please!

Figure 2.19

Paper pushers.

No need to start with an outline this time, just turn **Tracing Paper** opacity up to the maximum, 90%, so you see just enough of the source image to guide your brush. This will be a more detailed rendering than the first version. Apply your pastel strokes following the contours of the fruit and the bowl. Figure 2.20 shows the basic elements laid in.

Now you can work on details and accents. Tap the **Reset Tool** icon to return your brush to its original size. Enable **Clone Color** once again, and find a few areas to bring into somewhat sharper focus. Keep the source image visible at all times, referring to it frequently.

The challenge at this stage is to keep from getting too "tight" and simply reproducing the original photo. Also, it's tempting to rely on **Cloner** brushes too much. Remember to take control from time to time, using colors that you actually pick yourself! A good drawing will have a focal point or two, with other sections less important. Ways to reduce the visual impact of portions of your drawing include blurring, erasing, and altering color or contrast.

Figure 2.20
Pastel foundation.

Try blurring some of the edges of the fruit where it touches the bowl or another apple. The **Soft Blender Stump** or other **Blender** variant should do it. Erasing will be a problem if you used the **Paint Bucket** to create the background color. Instead, paint with the paper color, using one of the **Pastel** or **Chalk** variants. Most of the white highlights in the photo are too strong, so add some yellow strokes to tone them down a bit. Small details can be enhanced with the tiny **Pencil Sketch Cloner**, but some parts of the drawing, such as the crisp shine on the lip of the bowl, are much easier to create without cloning.

Figure 2.21, the finished drawing, includes all of the techniques discussed here. The cast shadow of the bowl was made with a very large pastel in just a couple of strokes.

You'll return to cloning techniques in future lessons, but I just couldn't wait to introduce you to this powerful set of features.

Figure 2.21
How do you like THEM apples?

What's Next?

Keep practicing your tonal drawing and crosshatch techniques, with or without the aid of **Clone Color**. There are source photos on the website that supports this book to serve as subjects for drawing and painting at whatever your skill level is. I also encourage you to go to the market and buy some nice fresh produce to work with. Make your own photos, but even better, set your hand-picked fruit or vegetable on a surface next to your computer and draw it live! Aim a spotlight on one side to get dramatic highlights and shadows.

After every lesson or practice session, choose your best couple of drawings and print them. That way you'll have tangible evidence of your work to hang on the walls. Over time you'll be able to observe your skills improving. Examining a print of your drawing is also a good way to evaluate it for possible changes. Most desktop inkjet printers can create high-quality output. To enhance the fine art nature of your image, use special paper or other media designed for your printer. High gloss heavy weight photo paper might be ideal for some projects, canvas or watercolor paper for others (see Appendix A for resources).

3 Have Another Layer

Regardless of subject matter or style, it's often a good idea to separate elements of your artwork into layers. For example, draw outlines on one layer and create color on another. You'll be able to make changes to one layer while other layers are protected. You can even shuffle layers around to experiment with alternate compositions and effects.

For this lesson, you'll use the following items from the website that supports this book:

- Images: **shoes-aerosole1.jpg**, **shoes-aerosole2.jpg**, **burlap.jpg**, and **aquarium.jpg**
- Custom palettes: **Shoes and Fish**

Comfortable Shoes

Open the **shoes_aerosole1.jpg,** found in the **Things** folder on the website that accompanies this book. Crop it to remove everything but the gray shoe in the foreground, as shown in Figure 3.1.

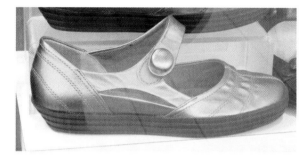

Figure 3.1

A sensible shoe.

Choose the **Real 6B Soft Pencil** from the custom palette for this lesson. Scribble on a blank canvas to get the feel of this Pencil variant.

Use **File > Quick Clone** to get access to tracing paper.

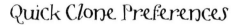

Quick Clone Preferences

Painter 12 added a section in **Preferences** devoted to customizing the **Quick Clone** environment. Settings for this project are: uncheck **Close Source Image** (this will leave the source image open) and **Switch to Cloner Brushes**. The other options should remain checked.

Using various shades of gray, make a sketchy drawing of the shoe, following the contours of the forms. If you want to fix a line, no need to switch to an eraser. Just use the **Option/Alt** key to get the **Dropper** function and click on the white background. Then "white-out" the lines you want to correct. Press **Option/Alt** once again to click on a black or gray pixel, and you're good to draw. Remember to use the **Page Rotate** tool to tilt the canvas for your comfort.

It's Been Real

Dry media (chalk, pencils, conte sticks, and pastels) that have the word **Real** in their names are capable of behaving in a realistic way when you tilt your stylus. Working with traditional dry media, you can make very wide marks when the stick or pencil is held at an extreme angle. Figure 3.2 shows several strokes made with the **Real 6B Soft Pencil**, using black and gray with the stylus held upright for a thin stroke and at various angles for broad lines. You can even change your grip to hold the stylus nearly parallel to the tablet, as shown in Figure 3.3, for the widest stroke possible—like drawing with the side of a piece of chalk!

Figure 3.2

"Real" pencil marks.

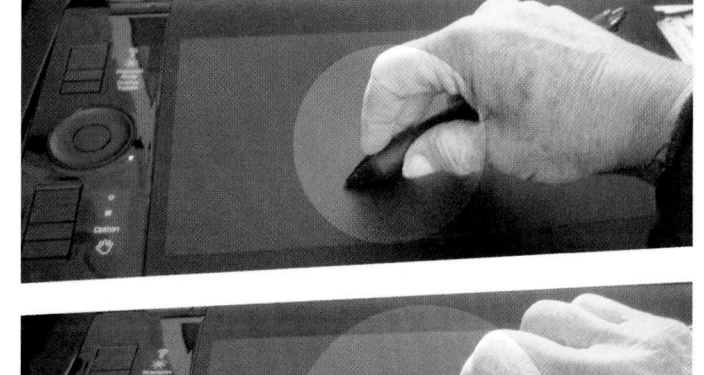

Figure 3.3

Real steep angle grips.

My drawing is shown in Figure 3.4. Save your sketch and keep it handy for later. You will draw two more shoes, using different brush variants and styles. Then you'll make a layered composite of all three drawings.

Open the **shoes_aerosole2.jpg** photo, shown in Figure 3.5. You'll be drawing the blue-gray flat shoe on the left, and also the beige suede open-toed number on the lower right. For convenience, make a separate image file for each of them.

Figure 3.4
Real sketchy.

Let's work on the blue-gray flat. Make a **Quick Clone** and choose the **Smooth Edge** variant from the custom palette for this lesson. It has a chisel shape that allows you to change the thickness of the line with the direction of your stroke. Take some practice "swings" with this brush, then make a bold graphic line drawing of the basic outlines of the shoe, similar to Figure 3.6. A low opacity for tracing paper, about 40%, is best when you draw with black, so you can see more of the source image. You can change the **Tracing Paper** opacity by using the slider in the **Clone Source** panel.

Figure 3.6
Simple lines.

Figure 3.5
Flats and heels.

Add a Color Layer

You'll add color on a separate layer. Make a new layer by tapping the **New Layer** icon at the bottom of the **Layers** panel, or choosing the **New Layer** command in the **Layers** menu. Sample a blue-gray color from the photo and switch to the **Flat Color** Pen in the second row of the custom palette. This variant makes a smooth fat stroke with a perfectly round beginning and end. There's no variation in pressure and no "grainy" response to paper texture. You can cover a lot of ground with one stroke of this pen. You'll also cover up what's on the canvas, unless you make this new layer transparent. Figure 3.7 shows the color layer added with **Flat Color**. The **Layers** panel in Figure 3.8 shows **Composite Method** is **Gel**, allowing the black lines to show through. **Multiply** or **Darken** methods will also work.

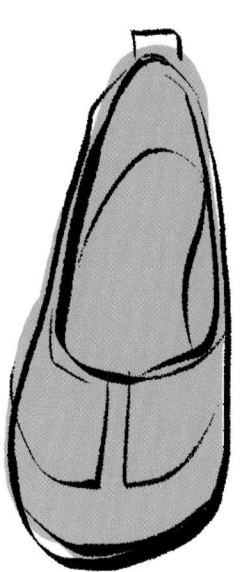

Figure 3.7
Flat color for flat shoe.

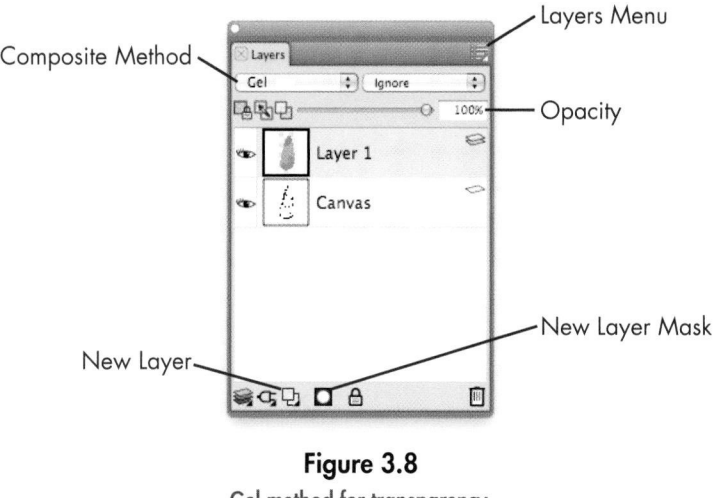

Figure 3.8
Gel method for transparency.

There's a Method to My Method

Composite Methods (corresponding, more or less, to Photoshop's Blending Modes) determine how a layer will interact with the canvas image or another layer under it. They always involve a comparison of the pixels between the two layers. For example, **Darken** method compares pixels and the darker of the two "wins." It's often a good idea to explore several **Composite Methods** as you develop a layered image. You may find some surprising and exciting effects.

Add a couple of **Flat Color** strokes with a darker blue-gray for quick shading. To create the textured area, switch to the **Square Hard Pastel** variant and find a paper that is similar to the fabric. I chose the **Fine Dots** paper, increasing its scale to about 125% in the **Papers** panel. The finished shoe appears in Figure 3.9.

Ready for the other shoe to drop? Make a rough sketch of the open-toed mid-heel shoe, using a dark brown color with the **Fine Tip Marker**. The sketch in Figure 3.10 is a good beginning.

Figure 3.9
A shoe-in.

Figure 3.10
Fine markings.

Sensitivity Training

Does it take too much pressure to make a line thicker or darker? Or is it difficult to make a delicate line, because you can't lighten up enough on the stylus? Well, it's not your fault. You just need to adjust the sensitivity of your Wacom stylus, using Painter's **Preferences > Brush Tracking** feature.

Add a new layer for color and texture. Use the **Dull Conte** with a light brown color. **Conte** variants imitate the French Conte sticks, and have a creamy look and feel. They are "grainy," meaning they reveal paper texture, so choose a subtle texture, such as **Raw Pulp** from the **Drawing Paper Textures** library. The look of suede depends on the way light is reflected from slight differences in the direction of the nap. This can be suggested effectively by dabbing some lighter and darker strokes with **Dull Conte** and smoothing them slightly with a **Blender** variant. The **Blender** provided in this custom palette is **Pointed Stump**. The finished suede shoe is shown in Figure 3.11.

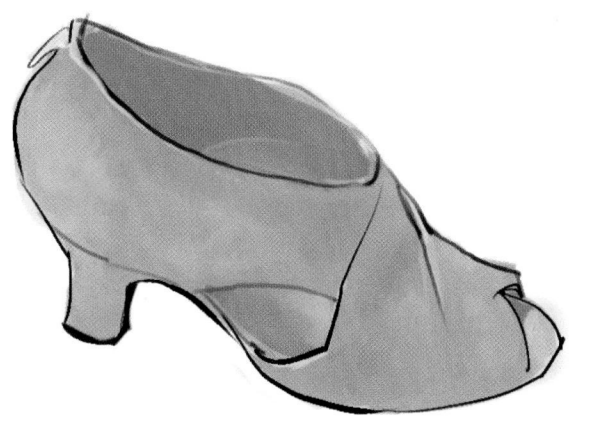

Figure 3.11

Don't step on my brown suede shoe.

Shoes for Industry

The three shoe drawings you made will be combined to create a composite that could work in an advertisement for Aerosole's spring line. The final image is shown in Figure 3.12, so you can see what you're aiming for. The **Layers** panel will look like Figure 3.13 at that point.

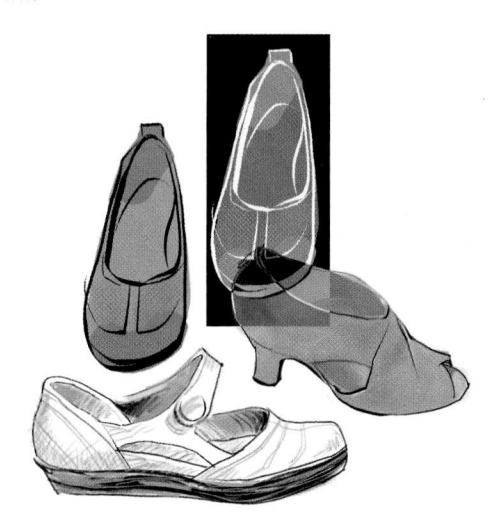

Figure 3.12

One shoe, two shoe, brown shoe, blue shoe.

Figure 3.13

Shoe stack.

Use the **Drop** command in the **Layers** menu to flatten each of the individual shoe images and use **File > Save As** to choose a new name and/or file format. Make a new white canvas with pixel dimensions 1250 wide by 1265 high, to accommodate all of the image elements. Use **Edit > Copy (Cmd/Ctrl+C)** followed by **Edit > Paste (Cmd/Ctrl+V)** to get all three of the shoe drawings into the new canvas, where each item will automatically create its own layer. Rename each layer by double-clicking its label in the **Layers** panel. Make another copy of the blue flat shoe layer by either pasting it twice, or using the **Duplicate Layer** command in the **Layers** menu at the top of your screen. Your layers should be stacked so that the gray strap shoe is at the bottom, and one of the blue flats is at the top. Stacking order can be changed by simply dragging the items in the **Layers** panel up or down.

The composite should look like Figure 3.14 at this point. The upper blue flat is blocking out some of the brown suede shoe because it is still using the default **Composite Method**. Change that to **Difference Method** for a dramatic effect.

To create a blue tint for the gray shoe, make another new layer and use the **Paint Bucket** to fill it with the blue-gray color you used earlier. Drag the solid color layer to a position just above the bottom shoe, where it will look just awful until you change **Composite Method** to **Overlay**.

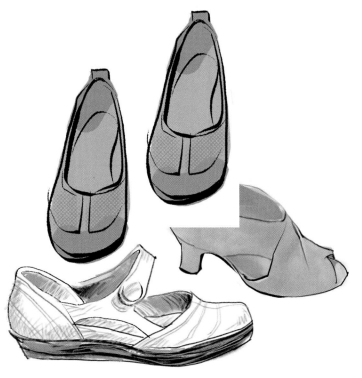

Figure 3.14

If the shoes fit...

Keep the layered image as a RIFF file in case you want to continue working on it. Painter also allows you to save layered files as Photoshop documents. To flatten your composite and save as a JPEG or in another file format, use the **Drop All** command in the **Layers** pop-up menu. More info on file formats can be found in Appendix A.

Papers, Please!

Let's take a break to do some paper work. A texture in Painter is simply a rectangular grayscale image element that repeats as a seamless tile. It carries no color information. You choose color whenever you use the selected paper with brush variants whose behavior is designed to express paper grain. Figure 3.15 shows the **Papers** panel, with a thumbnail of the currently active paper, **Linen Canvas**.

Painter provides a plethora of Paper libraries (that's just shy of a myriad), but there may be projects that call for custom textures. You can easily create a custom paper with commands in the **Papers** panel menu: **Make Paper** and **Capture Paper**.

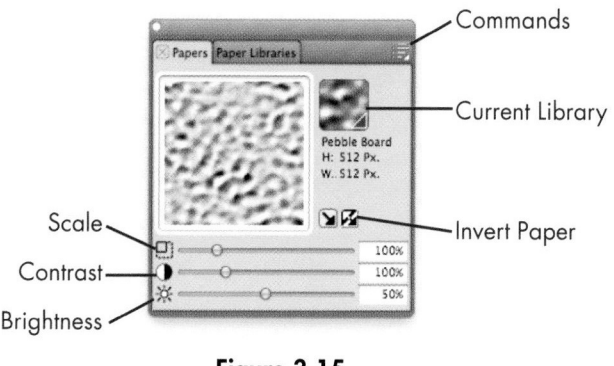

Figure 3.15
Show us your papers.

Gotcha!

Make Paper lets you produce a texture from a small list of geometric elements, such as lines or squares. **Capture Paper** requires making a selection on any open image and is much more fun. The "capture" feature is also available for making new brush tips, patterns, and icons. Anything you can surround with the marching ants of a selection marquee is up for "grabs!"

Use **File > New** to make a plain white canvas for creating and testing new paper textures. About 600 pixels square is fine, at any resolution. Make some small strokes and scribbles with several **Pen** variants, similar to Figure 3.16. Use dark gray for most of the marks, so the brightness and contrast of the resulting paper can be adjusted more easily. The purple strokes were made with the **Grad Pen**, which paints with the current **Gradient**. Color won't matter when a texture is generated.

Make a tight rectangular selection around your favorite scribble and use the **Capture Paper** command in the **Papers** panel pop-up menu. You'll be prompted to name your new paper, and it will instantly become part of the current library.

To create a texture from a photo, open the image **burlap.jpg**, shown in Figure 3.17. This should make a great paper texture after increasing the contrast. Use **Effects > Tonal Control > Brightness/Contrast** and move the contrast slider to the right. Drag a rectangular selection and use the **Capture Paper** command. Increase the **Crossfade** amount to about 50, as shown in Figure 3.18, to enhance the seamless effect.

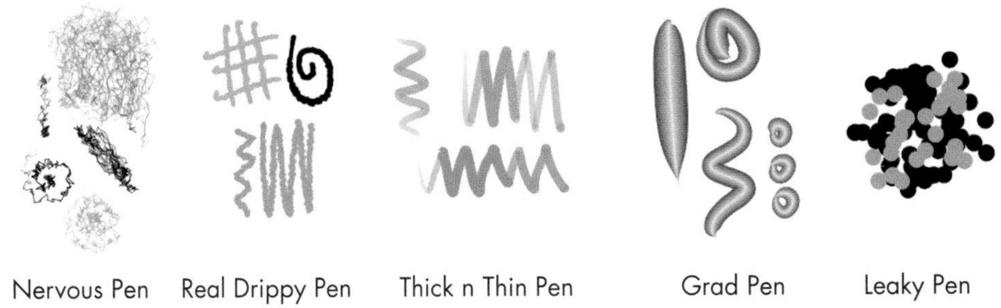

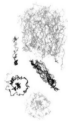

Nervous Pen
Real Drippy Pen
Thick n Thin Pen
Grad Pen
Leaky Pen

Figure 3.16
Squiggles, spirals, and drips.

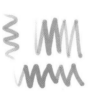

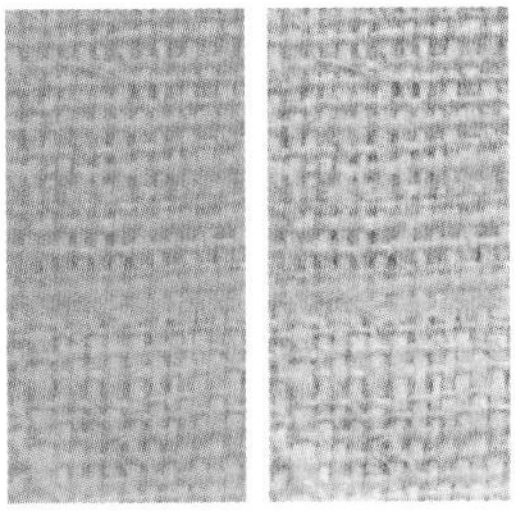

Figure 3.17
Burlap enhanced.

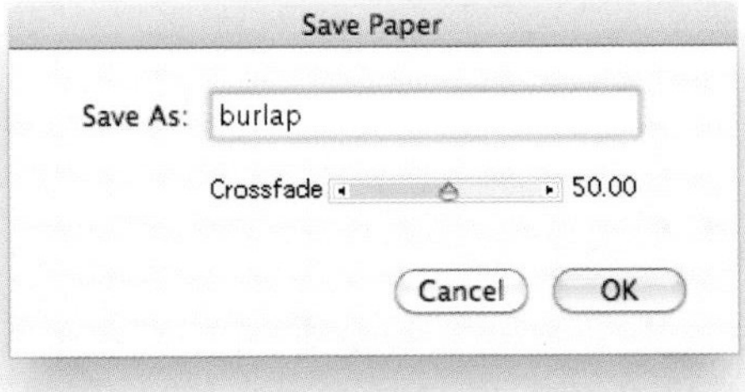
Save Paper
Save As:
burlap
Crossfade
50.00
Cancel
OK

Figure 3.18
Save Paper dialog box.

Use a **Hard Pastel** variant to test your new papers. Change the scale and invert the values for different looks. My efforts appear in Figure 3.19. The top row has a rectangle filled with **Nervous Pen** scribbles. I used the **Capture Paper** command to make a **Nervous Fibers** paper. The test stroke at the extreme right was made after inverting and also increasing the scale to 285%. The middle row shows the tiny purple donut I made with the **Grad Pen** as the captured element. The resulting paper responds wonderfully to changing pressure. This is the happy result of having the tile with built-in variation in tonality. The two-tone effect was made by inverting the paper and painting over the same area with a different color. Finally, in the last row, the texture was made from a photo or scan of real burlap.

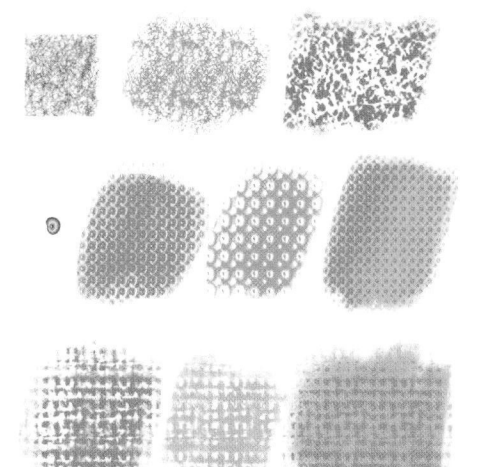

Figure 3.19

Three new papers.

Age of Aquariums

In this project you'll do more than just splash around with layers—you'll practically go snorkeling with them! So grab your mask and fins, and open the image **aquarium.jpg** from the **Nature** folder. Figure 3.20 shows the original image on the left and the same photo with **Watercolor Scheme** from the **Underpainting** panel applied on the right. You will find the **Underpainting** panel grouped with **Auto-Painting** panels.

Figure 3.20

Fishing for color.

Blending Layers

Suppose you want to combine the two versions, retaining the upper section of the original along with the vibrant new colors of the bottom half. You'll do just that with layers and that mask I mentioned. The following sequence of commands will create a new layer and place the altered version into it. Target the altered photo and use **Select > All (Cmd/Ctrl+A)** followed by **Edit > Copy (Cmd/Ctrl+C)**. Now target the original photo and use **Edit > Paste (Cmd/Ctrl+V)**. Look at the **Layers** panel to confirm that the operation was a success. Then create a layer mask by tapping the icon indicated at the bottom of the **Layers** panel, shown in Figure 3.21.

You'll use a black-to-white gradient in the layer mask to create a smooth blend between the layers. With black as the main color and white as the secondary color, open the **Gradient** panel and choose the **Two-Point** option. Figure 3.22 shows the angle necessary for the effect desired—a gradient starting with black at the top and gradually changing to white at the bottom. This will hide the upper portion of the altered layer, revealing the original. The fading of black to white will reveal more and more of the **Watercolor Scheme** version below it. Choose the **Paint Bucket** tool and make sure that **Gradient** is selected as the **Fill** option in the **Property Bar**. Then apply a fill to the layer mask.

New Layer Mask

Figure 3.21
Fish combo.

Who Was that Masked Layer?

A *layer mask* is a device for making portions of a layer visible or invisible, without actually erasing pixels or making any permanent changes to the image. White areas in the mask indicate 100% visibility, whereas black completely hides pixels. Shades of gray produce partial visibility.

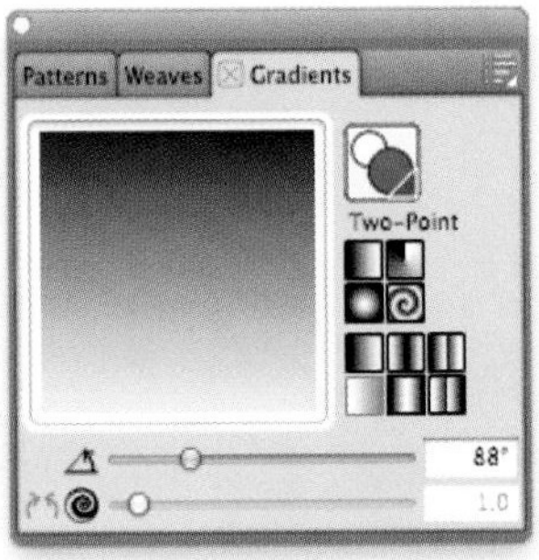

Figure 3.22
Your gradient is ready.

The fish in the upper two thirds of the image have lost some color vibrancy, because the layer is partially hidden. Painting with white in the layer mask will bring out the colorful fish. Use the **Smooth Round Pen** variant.

Brackets

If you want to fatten up the size of the pen for the bigger fish, use the right bracket key (]), which makes a brush bigger. To return the pen to its default size, use the left bracket key ([) or tap the **Reset Tool** icon in the **Property Bar**.

Figure 3.23 shows a detail of the finished composite before and after painting with white in the layer mask. Your **Layers** panel at this stage should look similar to Figure 3.24. Notice the tiny copy of the grayscale changes you made to manipulate visibility of the layer.

Figure 3.23

Fresh fish.

Figure 3.24

Fish layers.

When you're satisfied with the combination, use the **Drop** command in the **Layers** menu to commit to your changes and flatten the image. Use **Save As** to give your composite a new name, choosing the **RIFF** file format.

Serial Save

A great feature in both Painter 11 and 12 is **Iterative Save** in the **File** menu. Use it when you want to save stages in the development of a painting without breaking the flow in your creativity. The file format must be **RIFF**, Painter's default format. The keyboard shortcut **Option+Cmd+S** or **Alt+Ctrl+S** will save as you go. Changes will automatically be numbered in sequence.

Clone Fish

All of that was just preparation for a layered clone painting. Use **File > Quick Clone** to make a copy of the enhanced aquarium photo. Create a new layer and use it to make a black line drawing of the fish, leaving the rocks and water for later. Figure 3.25 shows my work at this stage, with tracing paper on at 50% opacity.

Figure 3.25

Fish lines.

Highlight the **Canvas** in your **Layers** panel. You'll use the three **Cloner** variants provided in the custom palette for this lesson to paint different sections of the image. All three of the **Cloner** variants use the same icon, because they are from the same brush category. Tap each one to see that they are, from left to right, **Smeary Bristle Cloner, Watercolor Run Cloner**, and **Impressionist Cloner**. Use the **Smeary Bristle Cloner** to paint the fish. Only a couple of strokes will be needed for each fish. Switch to the **Square Hard Pastel** and make it a **Cloner** by enabling **Clone Color** on the **Colors palette.** Figure 3.26 shows my results using **Pebble Board** texture for the water and **Worn Pavement** for the rocks. You may certainly choose different papers or create your own. The black line layer is not visible at the moment.

Iconography

It's easy to create a unique icon for any or all the items in your custom palette. See Lesson 6, "Customize Me!". Also, see the "Custom Brush Icons" tip in Lesson 5, "Be a People Person".

Figure 3.26
Fish rocks water.

Let's beef up the rocky area. **Watercolor Run Cloner** will do nicely. As soon as you use a **Watercolor** variant, a new layer dedicated to **Watercolor** strokes is created for you. Figure 3.27 shows the **Layers** panel at this point. **Watercolor** layers are automatically in **Gel** mode. Figure 3.28 shows a section of the image with the **Watercolor** cloning done.

Figure 3.27

Watercolor layer in Gel mode.

Figure 3.28

Rocks get darker.

There are several spots with a bit too much white showing. The **Impressionist Cloner** will handle those areas. Figure 3.29 shows how **Impressionist** strokes might look when cloning the entire image. Water looks great, but the fish seem like they've been through a blender.

With the background finished, turn your attention once again to the original black line layer. Are there ways to change how those lines interact with the rest of the painting? If you guessed changing **Composite Method,** you are correct. Figure 3.30 shows the finished painting, with splashes of color breaking up the solid black lines.

Figure 3.29

Choppy water and chopped fish.

Figure 3.30
Finny finish.

Here's how I did it. First, I just tried out several different **Composite Methods. Overlay** seemed the most promising, but the result wasn't quite strong enough to hold up against the background. I made a copy of the layer, using the **Duplicate Layer** command in the **Layers** drop-down menu. Once again, I just tried out several alternatives until **Saturation** method solved the problem. The effect is stronger with **Overlay** on top of **Saturation**, as the **Layers** panel in Figure 3.31 shows. The close-up detail in Figure 3.32 lets you compare all three stages—original, **Overlay** only, and **Overlay** plus **Saturation.**

This is just the kind of adventure I enjoy—plunging into unknown territory with very little chance of physical injury, unlike real-life snorkeling where you could easily scrape yourself against those rocks.

Figure 3.31
Two fishing lines.

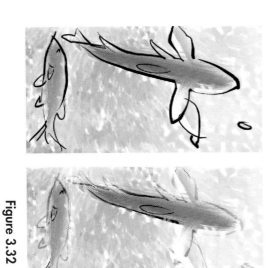

Figure 3.32
One fish, two fish.

What's Next?

Congratulations! You've covered the three "Fs"—fruit, fish, and footwear .

You've had considerable exposure to layers and layer masks. You explored composite methods enough to see how powerful they can be in the development of artwork. You learned to create custom paper textures from just about anything.

In the upcoming lessons, you'll work with a variety of subject matter, styles, and techniques. Brush controls will be introduced, so you can understand the anatomy of a Painter brush and how to bend it to your will. But first, grab some coffee and a snack. You earned it.

The Great 'scape

4

In this lesson you'll paint a couple of landscapes, but you won't have to worry about carrying sunscreen or rain gear. Later on you can pack a lunch with your laptop and set out for digital plein air painting in the park. But for now, enjoy the comfort and safety of home, protected from the criticism of nosy neighbors and rude tourists.

For this lesson, you'll use the following items from the website that supports this book:

- Images: **saguaro1.jpg** and **saguaro2.jpg**

- Custom palettes: **Arizona_Cacti.PAL** and **Airbrush_landscape.PAL**

Classic Western

Open the two images of saguaro cactus, found in the **Nature > Scenes** folder and shown in Figure 4.1.

Before you start drawing and painting, there's some image manipulation to do. Suppose you prefer the image on the left, but would like to add one of the cacti from the other image. Not a problem.

Figure 4.1
Saguaros (the "g" is silent).

Plants and Transplants

Use the **Lasso** tool to make a loose selection around the **saguaro2** cactus on the right, similar to Figure 4.2. Use **Edit > Copy (Cmd/Ctrl+C)**, and then target the **saguaro1** image and use **Edit > Paste (Cmd/Ctrl+V)** to give the cactus a new home on its own layer. The new layer is automatically created for you.

Position the new cactus where you want it. Make it larger, if needed, with the **Transform** tool, which shares a space with the **Layer Adjuster** tool. Figure 4.3 shows the bounding box and handles provided for transform operations. To constrain the proportions, hold down the **Shift** key as you drag a corner handle. **Transform** commands are also available in the **Edit** menu.

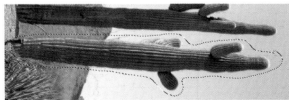

Figure 4.2
Rope it in.

You'll need to eliminate all those unwanted pixels around the cactus. Start by using the **Magic Wand** to select the bright blue sky pixels and delete them. Figure 4.4 shows the results. The remaining pixels can be erased, especially if you work carefully at the edge of the cactus. For a safety net, create a layer mask so you can make pixels invisible before you commit to deleting them altogether. Layer masks were used in Lesson 3, "Have Another Layer," but I'll remind you that painting with black on a layer mask hides pixels, and painting with white makes them visible again. A fine-point **Pen** variant works well. When you're satisfied with the results, use the **Drop** command to flatten the image and save it as a RIFF file, so you can use **Iterative Save (Cmd/Ctrl+Opt/Alt+S)** as the image develops.

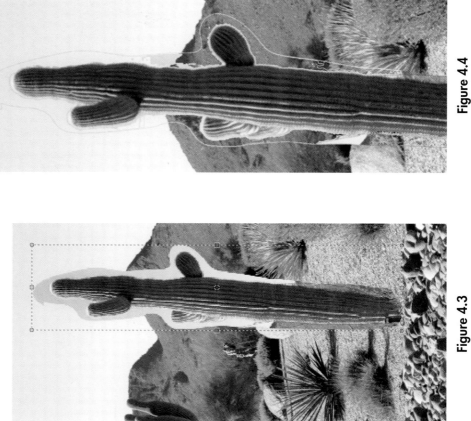

Figure 4.3
Drag it up.

Figure 4.4
Mask it out.

The top of the original cactus shoots through the top of the photo. If that bothers you, fix it. Make a loose **Lasso** selection, shown in the left side of Figure 4.5, with the shape you want for trimming the top of the cactus. Choose the **Airbrush** provided in the custom palette for this lesson—**Fine Tip Soft Air**. Sample the blue sky near the section you want to eliminate and paint over it. The right side of Figure 4.5 shows an intermediate state. Use the **Blur** variant of the **Blenders** to gently soften the edge of your new cactus tip.

Protected

Selected

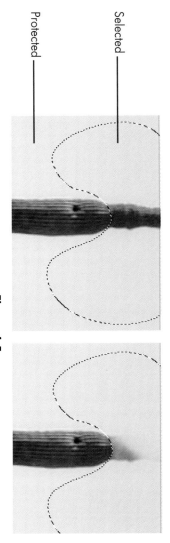

Figure 4.5
Trim it off.

Settings and Sets

Open the **Underpainting** panel, found in the **Auto-Painting Panels** group in the **Window** menu. Change the **Color Scheme** to **Sketchbook**. Create a soft, irregular edge using the jagged **Edge Effect** with the default amount of 25%. Those settings are shown in Figure 4.6. The prepared image, in Figure 4.7, has the look of a faded photo from a bygone era.

Figure 4.6
Tone it down.

Don't rely on **Clone Color** for this project. Instead, create a painting from scratch using the prepared photo as a reference. In order to restrict your color choices to those in the photo, make a custom color palette containing only those colors. That's easy. Open the **Color Sets** panel and choose **New Color Set from Image** from the pop-up menu of commands.

Figure 4.7
Rawhide!

Color Control

Choose a swatch in the current color set to change your main color for drawing and painting. A wide variety of alternate color sets can be loaded from the support files in your Painter application folder. You can also generate a custom set of colors from virtually any image source.

This new color set, shown in Figure 4.8, might look a bit different from yours until you change the way color swatches are displayed. I chose the medium swatch size from **Color Set Library View** in the pop-up menu. I also changed the sort order to **LHS** so that the swatches are arranged primarily according to lightness (L). Not all the swatches are showing here. Scroll up or down to see the darkest and lightest colors. There are some orangey shades in this set that were hard to notice in the image.

You'll develop your landscape painting in a traditional way, from simple lines and shapes to more complexity and detail. Each stage will be on a separate layer, allowing you to gradually minimize earlier stages by reducing their opacity.

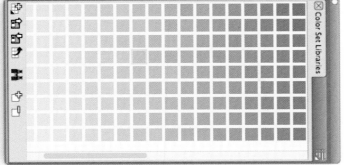

Figure 4.8
Home on the color range.

Line, Shape, and Tone

Make a blank canvas about the same size as the photo. (To find the pixel dimensions of an image, choose **Resize** from the **Canvas** menu.) Analyze the composition of the prepared photo according to four elements—line, shape, tone, and texture. Make a new layer and roughly lay out the basic lines in pencil. There are two major vertical lines for the cacti, two slightly angled horizontal lines establishing different sections of foreground and a wavy line for the distant mountains. Include a line showing the edges. Don't get any more detailed than the sketch in Figure 4.9.

Those lines also establish the basic shapes. Add another new layer for large areas of tonality. Use either **Gel** or **Multiply** method to allow the line layer to show through. Medium brown and creamy yellow, applied with a **Chunky Oil Pastel**, divide the picture plane into light (white paper), dark, and midtones. Figure 4.10 shows the basic image layout.

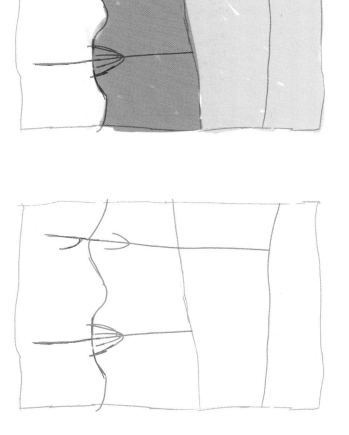

Figure 4.9
Starting lines.

Figure 4.10
Roughing it.

Tool Marks

There is a rich variety of texture in the source image—vertical ridges of the cacti, spiky and bristly elements of the smaller plants, fine-grained gravel, and chunky stones. Use **Pebble Board** paper with **Chunky Oil Pastel** to suggest the stones in the foreground. For the distant mountains reduce the scale of **Pebble Board** in the **Papers** panel. Figure 4.11 shows the **Papers** panel with settings for changing the size and other qualities of a texture. An interesting paper choice for the trees and some bushes is **Retro Fabric**.

Just Add Paper

The custom palette for this project includes a couple of paper swatches as well as brush variants, to save you time rummaging through paper libraries. You can even include frequently used commands in a custom palette. Use **Custom Palette > Add Command** from the **Window** menu.

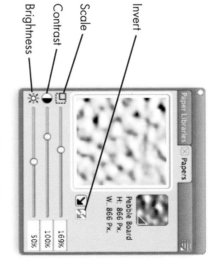

Invert

Scale

Contrast

Brightness

Figure 4.11
Papers controls.

Figure 4.12 shows the saguaros and some smaller shapes fleshed out with just a few **Oil Pastel** strokes. You can erase most of the original line layer at this point, but keep the outline of the edge, which is important for the composition.

The tonality layer is now your primary layer for developing the drawing. Make a copy of it with the **Duplicate Layer** command. Use the **Default Composite Method** to cover up the layers below. Now you can work on the copy while the current state remains untouched, as a safety net.

Continue to develop the forms with the paper textures suggested or others that you prefer. For the foreground stones **Pebble Board** is ideal. Change its scale several times and apply it with **Square Hard Pastel** for stronger texture. Invert the paper and use lighter colors for the sunlit surfaces. To give the distant mountains more depth, use **Hard Pastel** with **Artists Rough Paper**, blending here and there with the **Flat Grainy Stump**. Define the bushes in the middle distance with lighter and darker colors using the **Retro Fabric** texture once again.

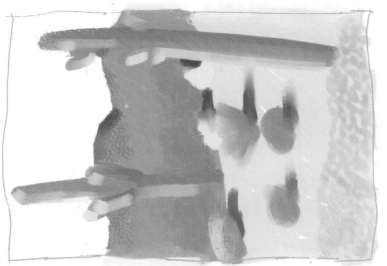

Figure 4.12
Texture added.

Safety first

Making copies of a layer is just one way to save stages in your work. **Iterative Save (Cmd/Ctrl+Opt/Alt+S)** is an excellent option if you want to have a series of versions as separate files. It's a good idea to add the **Iterative Save** command to any custom palette. **File > Clone** can also allow you to continue working while the current state is preserved.

Figure 4.13 shows the drawing at this stage. I added a pale yellow sky to define the upper edges so I could eliminate the outline layer.

The **Nervous Pen** is a quirky variant that could be just right for the prickly vertical striations in the two main characters. Choose the dark browns and greens for the shadow side and bright yellow or white for the sunlit parts. Figure 4.14 shows a close-up of the right cactus with **Nervous Pen** strokes applied.

Too Much Caffeine?

Nervous Pen behaves as it does because of its **Jitter** setting. **Jitter** is one of many variables that determine the behavior of a variant. See Lesson 6, "Customize Me!," for much more about brush controls.

Figure 4.13
Just desert.

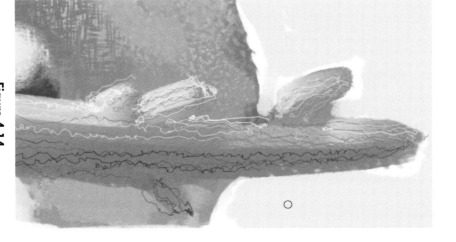

Figure 4.14
Nervous energy.

For finishing touches to your Arizona landscape, as shown in Figure 4.15, use a **Pencil** or decaffeinated **Pen** to add some spiky lines to the bushes. The smoothness of the sky and fine-grained gravel give the eyes a place to rest.

Figure 4.15
Now I can write off my trip to Phoenix.

Imaginary Landscape

In traditional airbrush painting, portions of the paper or other support are protected from paint or ink with a mask. These can be made from tape or cardboard or self-adhesive frisket paper cut to the precise shape needed. It shouldn't surprise you that for digital airbrush art, creating masks is much easier.

Pixel-based applications like Painter and Photoshop provide several tools for selecting portions of the canvas to accept painted strokes or effects. Whatever isn't selected is, by definition, masked. You can make perfect rectangles and ovals, or draw freehand selections around an irregular area using the **Lasso** tool. The **Polygon Lasso** tool is handy for selecting shapes with straight edges. A sophisticated selection tool that has no counterpart in traditional media is the **Magic Wand**, which selects all pixels in a defined color range. Figure 4.16 shows where the selection tools are located on the **Toolbox.** Notice the **Selection Adjuster** tool, which allows you to move or alter a selection marquee. The **Property Bar** shows that the **Polygon Lasso** is currently active. Choices are available for adding to or subtracting from a selection using any of the selection tools. This allows you to create some very complex selection areas.

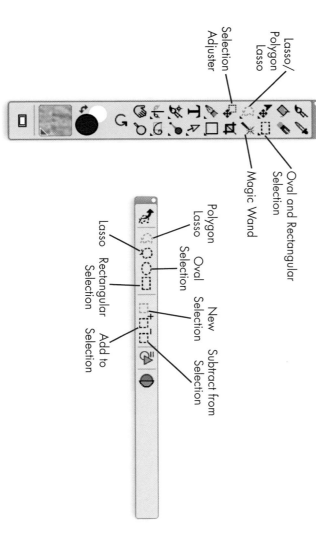

Lasso/
Polygon
Lasso

Selection
Adjuster

Oval and Rectangular
Selection

Magic Wand

Polygon
Lasso

Oval
Selection

New
Selection

Subtract from
Selection

Lasso

Rectangular
Selection

Add to
Selection

When the Ants Come Marching In

An active selection is surrounded by a marquee that looks like an animated dashed line. The cute nickname for this is *marching ants*. You might want to turn off the marching ants (without losing the selection) to see your work better. The **Hide/Show Marquee** toggle in the **Select** menu has a keyboard shortcut: **Shift+Cmd/Ctrl+H**.

You can apply paint to a selection without having to be careful at the edges. You can also use the **Paint Bucket** tool to fill a selection instantly with your choice from the **Property Bar**: current color, gradient, pattern, or weave. An especially dandy command in the **Select** menu is **Stroke Selection**. This will automatically paint the edges of your selection with the current color, using the current brush variant.

Air Apparent

The ideal brush category for working with selection masks is *airbrushes*. Traditional airbrushes spray tiny droplets of pigment mixed with compressed air. The instrument connected to that compressed air source is a device with a nozzle and a small reservoir for pigment. It has a couple of tiny wheels for finger control of the size of the spray and the density and coarseness of the droplets. It takes quite a bit of practice to get skilled with a traditional airbrush. Painter lets you shave months, even years, off that process.

Make a new canvas for trying out several of the **Airbrush** variants. Figure 4.17 includes some **Broad Wheel** strokes at the upper left. Airbrushes respond not only to pressure but also to the tilt of your Wacom stylus, creating a realistic directional spray of pigment. Next is the aptly named **Graffiti** variant, which can produce a directional spraycan effect as well as controlled drawing or lettering. **Variable Splatter** has clumpy droplets of different sizes. The multi-colored effect is made by adding **Color Variability** to the spatter. Painter 12 groups the **Color Variability** panel, shown in Figure 4.18, with the other **Brush Control** panels found in the **Window** menu.

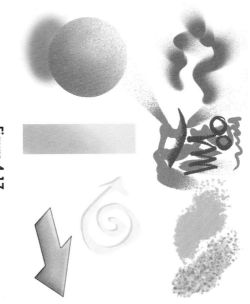

Figure 4.17

Practice, practice.

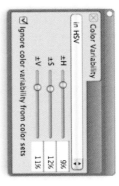

Figure 4.18

Hue, saturation, and value variations.

Various Variables

NEW 12

Painter 12 provides more ways to make color variation in a stroke than just fiddling with **Hue, Saturation,** and **Value (HSV)**. You can choose the colors in a gradient or a color set to create some unusual effects, as shown in Figure 4.19.

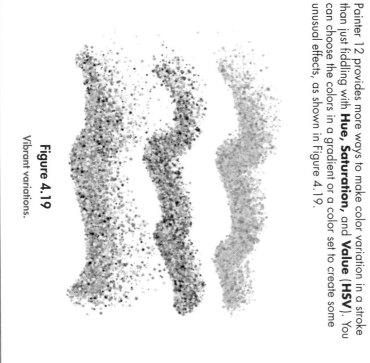

Figure 4.19

Vibrant variations.

Try spraying both inside and outside a selection with different colors. The golden sphere shown in Figure 4.17 was made with a circular selection—the **Oval Selection** tool is constrained into a perfect circle with the **Shift** key. Paint inside the circle with the **Coarse Spray**, using golden yellow followed by a lighter yellow near the top and brown at the bottom, The cast shadow requires using the **Select > Invert Selection** command to protect the circle and paint outside it. The **Digital Airbrush** variant, a much finer spray, was used for the shadow. The green rectangle, also painted with the **Digital Airbrush** variant, shows that with a little practice you can create smooth gradients "by hand."

Painter provides a library of ready-made selections of symbols, arrows, hearts, and much more. Find them in **Media Library** panels. A library of selections is shown in Figure 4.20. Double-click one of them and it will appear on your canvas instantly, ready for you to experiment with. Users of earlier versions will find the **Selection Portfolio** under the **Window** menu; the items need to be dragged to your canvas. That curly arrow was painted with a teal blue, then the selection was moved a few pixels up and to the right with the **Selection Adjuster**. A lighter tint was sprayed on to create the depth effect. A soft highlight and shadow on the pink arrow were made with the 30-pixel **Soft Airbrush**. For a thin outline, switch to the 5-pixel **Tiny Soft Air** and use the **Stroke Selection** command.

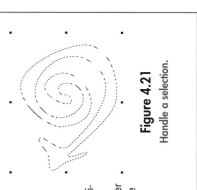

Figure 4.20
A collection of selections.

Figure 4.21
Handle a selection.

Major Adjustments

Use the **Selection Adjuster** not only to move a selection, but to resize, distort, and rotate it. When you choose the **Selection Adjuster** tool and click on an active selection, eight tiny black handles will appear, as shown in Figure 4.21. Drag the appropriate handle to scale the selection, with or without maintaining its proportions. To tilt a selection, press the **Cmd/Ctrl** key and hover your stylus over a corner handle until the cursor becomes a rotate symbol. Then drag the handle to any angle you desire.

Prepare to Pretend

Create a whimsical world from your imagination, using only **Airbrush** variants and selection maneuvers. Start by making a very rough sketch, similar to the one in Figure 4.22. You'll develop it into an illustration appropriate for a children's book. Use your sketch as a jumping-off place, but don't feel confined by it.

The custom palette for this project, shown in Figure 4.23, has six **Airbrush** variants with identical icons. The first thing you'll want to do is find a way to tell them apart. Happily, customizing icons in Painter 12 is quick and easy.

Figure 4.23
Iconic wallpaper?

Make a stroke with each of the **Airbrush** variants, similar to Figure 4.24, using a different color for each. Drag a small rectangular selection to represent a variant whose icon you want to replace—in this case it is **Variable Splatter** on the lower right. Right-click (**Ctrl**-click on the Mac) the target item in the custom palette. Choose **Capture Custom Icon** from the pop-up list of options. That's all there is to it! Repeat with an appropriate capture for each of the other items in the custom palette, which will end up looking something like Figure 4.25. The original color will be revealed when your stylus hovers over an icon.

Figure 4.25
Hover over splatter.

Figure 4.22
'Shrooms and butterflies.

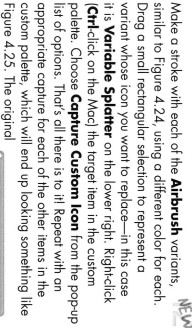

NEW

Coarse
Spray

Digital
Airbrush

Soft
Airbrush

Fine Tip
Soft Air

Tiny
Soft Air

Variable
Splatter

Figure 4.24
Strokes for capture.

To create a special set of colors for this project, use the **New Color Set** option on the **Color Set Libraries** panel. After you give it a name, begin to sample colors you like from your sketch, or choose them in the **Color** panel. Each time you change the current color, click the **Add Color To Color Set** icon. Repeat until you have all the colors you want added. Of course you can add more colors as needed, or remove some of them with the **Delete Color** icon. My color set for this project is shown in Figure 4.26.

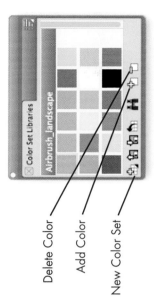

Delete Color

Add Color

New Color Set

Figure 4.26
Custom colors.

Mythical Mastery Tour

Make a new white canvas the size and resolution you want. Paper texture won't matter, because **Airbrush** variants ignore it. Begin with the hill in the foreground. Drag a large oval selection horizontally as far as you can. You'll still need to enlarge it beyond the image edges, using the **Selection Adjuster**, as shown in Figure 4.27.

Use the **Coarse Spray** airbrush and two shades of blue-green to paint the hill. Use **Select > Save Selection** and give the selection a descriptive name, as shown in Figure 4.28. Save each new selection with a unique name as you work.

Figure 4.27
Stretch beyond the edges.

Figure 4.28
Select and save.

Each of the stripes on the hill requires a freehand selection made with the **Lasso** tool. Don't worry if it's not perfect—you can fix it. Press the **Shift** key as you use the **Lasso** for the second and third stripe, so they will be added to your first one, and then use **Save Selection**. Open the **Channels** panel, which should look similar to Figure 4.29 at this point.

Make the Stripes channel visible. If you turn off visibility of the RGB image (the blue hill), the channel will appear as black and white, where white indicates the portion that is inside the selection. When the RGB image is visible, the channel appears as semi-transparent red (the masked or unselected area corresponding to black) and clear (corresponding to white). Both views are shown in Figure 4.30.

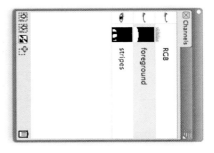

Figure 4.29
Channeling stripes.

Your friend the Channel

When you save a selection you are automatically creating an Alpha channel that stores information as an image with white indicating selected pixels and black representing unselected pixels. Partial selections, such as a feathered edge, appear as shades of gray. This is similar to using a layer mask for hiding and revealing pixels in a layer. Masks and channels can be altered by painting black, white, or gray into them. It is often easier to improve a selection by painting on the channel than by working entirely with selection tools.

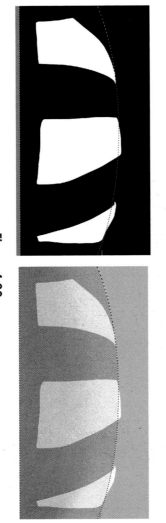

Figure 4.30
Channels are also masks.

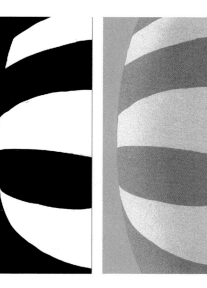

Figure 4.31

Fix for a mask is fit for a channel.

In Figure 4.30, I must have made the **Lasso** selections when the image window did not reveal the entire painting. It's clear that my effort requires considerable repair. Luckily, that's not hard. Using either view and a **Pen** variant you can control easily, such as the **Scratchboard Tool** pen, paint white where you want to add to the selection (extending the stripes to the edges) and black where you want to subtract from it (trimming off pixels that extend above the hill). Figure 4.31 shows the fix.

Continue by systematically creating, painting, and saving selections. I decided to make that middle section of pale green into a cliff on the left, with a gently undulating waterfall. They were both painted with the **Digital Airbrush** and **Soft Airbrush** in several shades of blue and green. Figure 4.32 shows the left side of the artwork. The **Channels** panel at this point is shown in Figure 4.33.

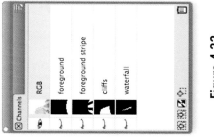

Figure 4.33

Channels for all.

Figure 4.32

Cliff and falls.

Fabulous Foliage

With the cliff on the left, let's put all the trees on the right. The trunks are each made with a thin vertical rectangular selection, filled at various angles with the **Selection Adjuster**. They get a two-tone coat of paint with the **Digital Airbrush**. Turn trees into lollipops by using spirals from a **Selection Portfolio**. Spray a contrasting color behind each one by inverting the selection and painting with the 30-pixel **Soft Airbrush** variant. The results are displayed in Figure 4.34.

Figure 4.34
New species of flora.

Return your attention to the foreground once again, and make a couple of mushrooms. The mushroom cap starts with a vertical oval and the bottom is subtracted from it with a selection rectangle, shown in Figure 4.35. Use either the **Subtract from Selection** button in the **Property Bar** or press the **Option/Alt** key. The stems are either rectangular or **Polygon Lasso** selections.

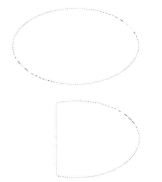

Figure 4.35
Fresh fungi.

Stripes on the yellow mushroom were painted freehand with the dainty **Tiny Soft Air**. To make dimensional bumps on the red mushroom, use small oval selections. Recall the highlight and shadow technique from your practice earlier. The insect in the foreground? You could make it from scratch with a tiny oval added to a **Polygon Lasso** selection, but I simply dragged an exclamation point from a **Selection Portfolio**, added the highlight and drop shadow as usual, and then painted the legs with **Tiny Soft Air**.

To Air is Human

Up in the sky, apply pale blue with the **Digital Airbrush,** allowing it to fade out as it reaches the lollipop trees. Make a puffy cloud selection with the **Lasso.** Fill with white and add depth by shading the bottom edge of the cloud as well as a hint of yellow at the top. The second cloud uses the same selection, just reduced in size. Butterflies, as you might have guessed, are made with the same freehand **Lasso** selection, altered with the **Selection Adjuster**. The finished art is shown in Figure 4.36.

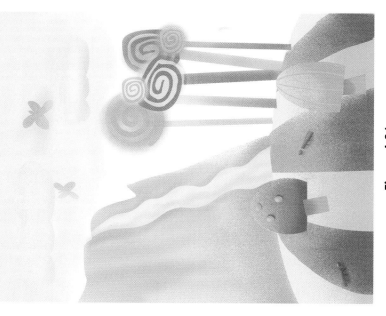

Figure 4.36
Fantasy fulfillment!

You (or your client) might want to make changes later. As long as you save the image file in a format that preserves the alpha channels, that's not a problem. **RIFF**, **PSD**, and **TIFF** will work nicely. Suppose you want to change the cliff area. Use **Select > Load Selection**, choosing **Cliff**. Then, subtract the waterfall and mushroom cap, by loading each of them and choosing the operation **Subtract From Selection**, as shown in Figure 4.37.

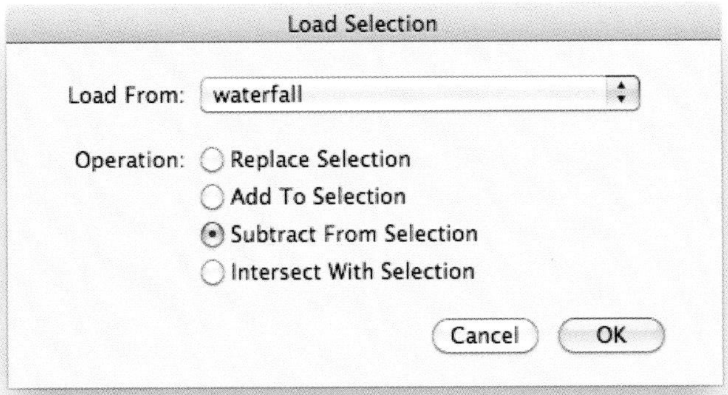

Figure 4.37
Dehydrated.

Create a different look for the cliff with the **Variable Splatter** airbrush. Before you spray, give the brush some color variability (see Figure 4.18). Figure 4.38 shows the effect of applying green spatters with **HSV** variation, followed by a few splats with color variation based on the current color set. Clumps of wild flowers in the distance are suggested.

Your Very Own Variant

If you want the changes you make to a brush to be permanent, you can create a new variant with your custom settings. **Brushes > Save Variant** lets you give the new brush a descriptive name, and adds it to the list of choices for the category. For example, save the **Variable Splatter** airbrush with color variability as **Variable Color Splatter**.

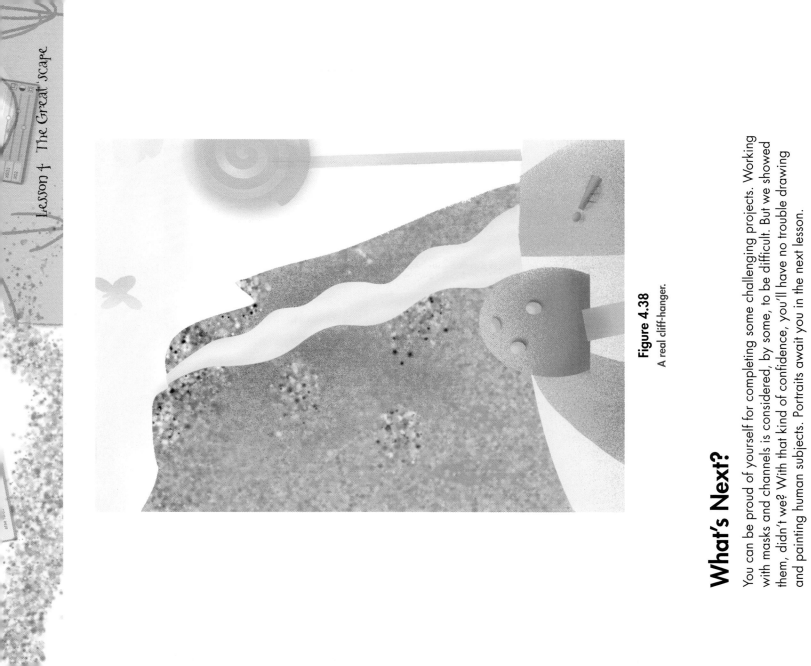

Figure 4.38
A real cliff-hanger.

What's Next?

You can be proud of yourself for completing some challenging projects. Working with masks and channels is considered, by some, to be difficult. But we showed them, didn't we? With that kind of confidence, you'll have no trouble drawing and painting human subjects. Portraits await you in the next lesson.

5 Be a People Person

Since the previous version of this book was published I have spent considerable time painting portraits in "messy media," —oils at first and then switching to acrylic. Capturing the likeness of a person is a much bigger challenge than making an apple look like a Granny Smith. Tracing and cloning a photo will handle the essential matters of accuracy and proportion. Beyond that is a vast array of choices for interpreting your subject. You'll get some practice doing just that in the following projects.

I have been fascinated with drawing and painting the human face and form for my entire career, so I'm pretty excited about this lesson.

For this lesson, you'll use the following items from the website that supports this book:

- Images: **Hines_guitar.jpg, Betsy_profile.jpg, Jan.jpg,** and **Cloner_icons.jpg**

- Custom palette: **Smear & Pick**

Warm-Up Pose

A portrait can be restricted to the head of a subject, but can also include the entire body. Open the photo **Hines_guitar.jpg**, shown in Figure 5.1. This image already has a good composition and an interesting arrangement of tones and shapes, with a minimal amount of color range. Load the custom palette **Smear & Pick**, using the **Import** command in the **Custom Palette Organizer**.

When you start with a blank canvas or sheet of paper, the first step might be to roughly establish the main shapes or the darkest and brightest areas. That's the first thing you'll do to this photo, by smearing away all the detail with a large **Blender** variant, until all that remains are the basic shapes and tones. Use strokes that follow the contours of the shapes, more or less, and vary the length and direction of your smears. After a few strokes, use **Save As** to give the image a new name. I produced the simplified version shown in Figure 5.2 using the **Pointed Stump**, included in the custom palette for this project. It's still a black man in white pants playing the guitar, but it's not Hines anymore. If you smeared so much that even the pose is gone, fear not.

Figure 5.1
The Artist Hines (that's his legal name).

Figure 5.2
The Artist Who?

Take a close look at the **Smear & Pick** custom palette, with its items labeled in Figure 5.3. Knowing what each of these tools can do will reveal the strategy for this painting. The **Pointed Stump**, as you have seen, creates bold, smooth smears between adjacent colors. The other blender variant is **Grainy Water**, for smaller and more controlled smearing. **Chalk Cloner** will enable you to "pick" out details from the original photo and add them back seamlessly, provided you choose a fine-grained paper texture. The **Soft Cloner** brings back the original pixels exactly, in case you want to start from scratch in some sections. **Soft Oil Pastel** will be useful to add painted areas that are not found in the photo. Finally, the **Fade** command, from the **Edit** menu, is handy to soften the effect of your previous stroke—it is a partial undo, at the percentage you choose.

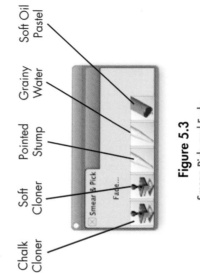
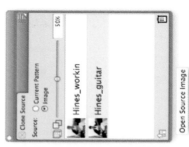

Chalk Cloner   Soft Cloner   Pointed Stump   Grainy Water   Soft Oil Pastel

Figure 5.3
Smear, Pick, and Fade.

Source Material

Open the **Clone Source** panel if it's not already showing and use the **Open Clone Source** icon at the bottom left to find the original photo (it went away when you saved the smeary version with another name). The **Clone Source** panel is shown in Figure 5.4, after the **Hines_guitar** photo has been added to the list.

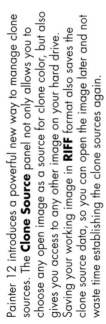

Figure 5.4
Resource management.

Reconsider the Source

Painter 12 introduces a powerful new way to manage clone sources. The **Clone Source** panel not only allows you to choose any open image as a source for clone color, but also gives you access to any other image on your hard drive. Saving your working image in **RIFF** format also saves the clone source data, so you can open the image later and not waste time establishing the clone sources again.

Use the **Chalk Cloner** to bring back some details in the important areas—the face, hands, and a hint of the guitar structure. Easy does it, because you'll want to have the entire painting make visual sense. Develop the painting with any combination of smearing, cloning, and fading. You may want to change the size of your brush from time to time.

Sizing and Resizing

The size of a brush can be changed in three ways.

1. You can use the slider in the **Property Bar**, guessing what the results will be.

2. For small changes, use the bracket keys: the left bracket ([]) reduces the size by a pixel or two, depending on your settings in the **General Preferences** for **Brush Size Increment.** As you'd expect, the right bracket ([]) increases size.

3. For on-the-fly changes while you are painting, hold down the **Cmd+Option (Ctrl+Alt)** keys and drag the "green thing" shown in Figure 5.5 to the size you prefer.

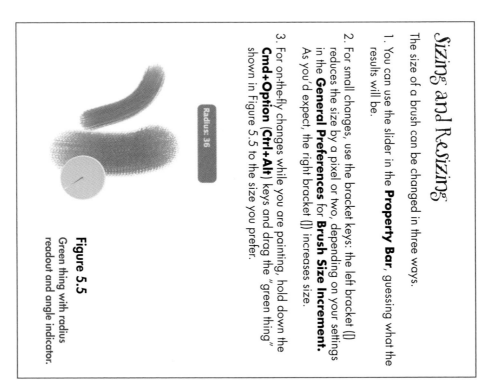

Radius: 36

Figure 5.5
Green thing with radius readout and angle indicator.

Don't try to copy my brushwork, but do use the images in Figures 5.6 through 5.11 as guides for your progress. Figure 5.7 shows a stage that has the lower edge of the guitar too crisp for my taste. Instead of smearing it again, I chose to use the previous version as the clone source, and paint the smears back with the **Soft Cloner.**

Figure 5.6
Some details emerge.

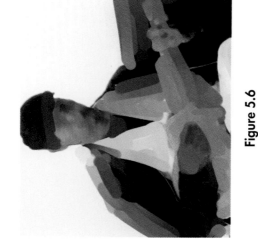

Figure 5.7
Too much information.

Trouser Material

I'm satisfied with the results, but now I notice that the big off-white areas at the top of the image are too empty. Let's liven them up by adding some of the light tints from Hines' clothing. A custom color set will help. Make a rectangular selection on the trouser legs, as shown in Figure 5.8. Choose **New Color Set from Selection** in the **Color Set Libraries** pop-up menu. The color set that is created, shown in Figure 5.9, has an array of soft pinks, mauves, and greens.

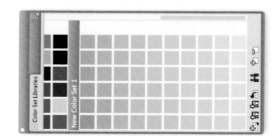

Figure 5.9
Way off-white.

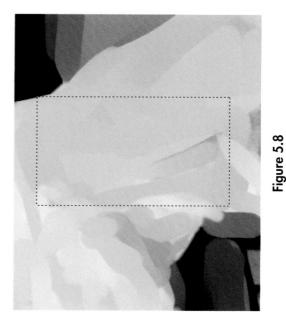

Figure 5.8
Lighter shades of pale.

Switch to the **Soft Oil Pastel** and use the new color set to paint parts of the white background, starting at the outer edges, similar to Figure 5.10. Smear and blend those strokes toward the center. Figure 5.11 shows my finished painting.

Figure 5.10
Background interest.

Figure 5.11
Classical guitar.

Face Time

The photo of Betsy in Figure 5.12 shows a redhaired woman posed in strong sunlight against a yellow brick wall.

I recently completed a 32×24 inch acrylic painting of Betsy on canvas, part of a series called "Gurls with Curls," expressive portraits of curly haired women. That painting is shown in Figure 5.13. If you criticize it for not being quite right around the mouth, I'd have to agree, but I was much more interested in painting that marvelous hair! Join me in creating a digital version. You won't attempt to imitate the results of the "real" painting, but you will definitely have fun with the hair. Open **Betsy_profile.jpg**.

Figure 5.12
Red hair and yellow bricks.

Figure 5.13
Betsy in messy media.

Mixing Media

There are many ways to "cross-pollinate" your digital and traditional artwork.

■ A digital piece can be reinterpreted on canvas or paper.

■ Reverse the above, as you are doing with Betsy in this section.

■ Take photos of each stage in a traditional painting and explore the next steps in Painter.

■ Print parts of a digital painting on thin Japanese paper and adhere them to your canvas or panel as part of a "real" collage.

The *Best Layered Plans*

The basic plan is to make several versions of the Betsy photo, by applying a different effect to each copy of the original. Then you'll paint with **Cloner** brushes, switching the clone source from one version to another. The image I ended up with is shown in Figure 5.14. Your mileage may vary, and it should.

Figure 5.14
Digital curls.

Make four identical layers of the original in one image file. Start by choosing **Select > All (Cmd/Ctrl+A)**, then **Edit > Paste (Cmd/Ctrl+V)**. Either repeat the **Paste** command three more times or choose the **Duplicate Layer** command three times, and your **Layers** panel should look like Figure 5.15.

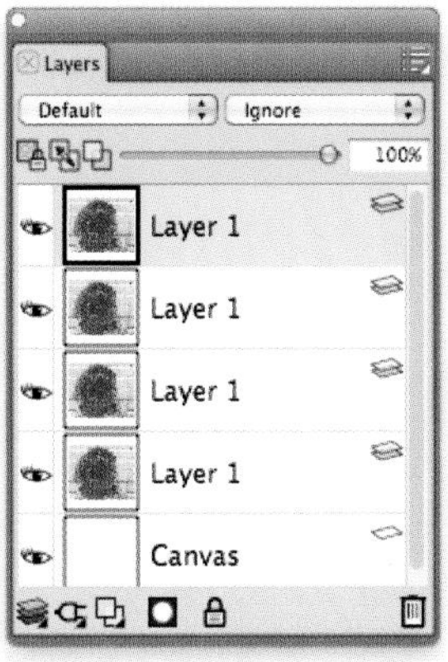

Figure 5.15
Layered faces.

Target the uppermost layer and apply **Effects > Surface Control > Sketch**, using settings similar to those in Figure 5.16. The results are too sketchy (even for me!), so I used **Edit > Fade** to bring back the original by 50%. Figure 5.17 shows the outcome—lighter colors and great texture, especially in her hair.

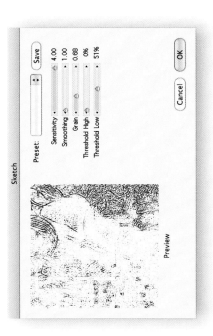

Figure 5.16
Ready, set, sketch!

Figure 5.17
Hair with more body.

Color Scheming

Apply the following effects to the remaining layers in any order; just be sure to turn off the visibility of other layers (by clicking on the eye icons) to see your results. An intriguing way to add wild color effects to an image is to apply a **Gradient** color ramp. Choose **Vivid Mixture** from the **Gradient Selector,** shown in Figure 5.18, and use the **Express in Image** command in the pop-up menu. You'll need to adjust the **Bias** slider, as shown in Figure 5.19, to map the values of the gradient to the values of your image. The preview thumbnail shows changes in value mapping as you move the slider around. A **Bias** around 64 will maintain most of the original distribution of values for the result in Figure 5.20.

Figure 5.18
Don't stare at this too long.

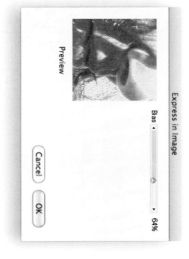

Figure 5.19
Can you be unbiased?

Figure 5.20
Flaming red hair.

Use **Effects > Surface Control > Apply Screen** on another layer. The dialog box shown in Figure 5.21 lets you choose any three colors as well as the method for using the effect. Choose **Image Luminance** rather than **Paper** or any of the other options. You don't have to use my colors, but the ones you do choose should be darkest on the left and lightest on the right, in order to maintain value mapping. The two **Threshold** sliders let you determine the value points where colors change. After clicking OK, I faded the effect slightly (25%) for the image shown cropped in Figure 5.22.

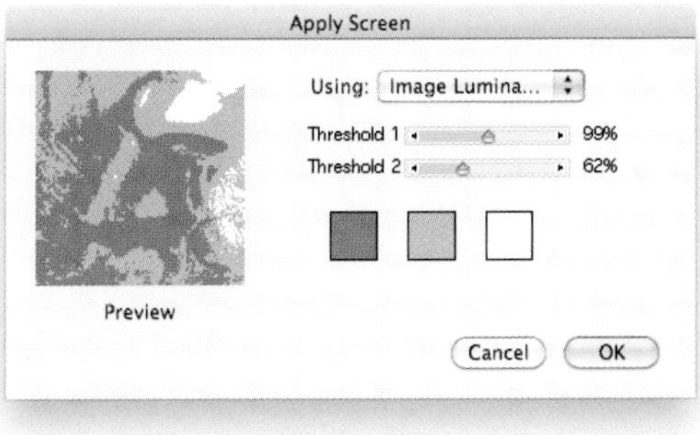

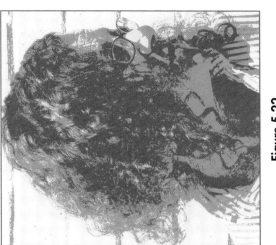

Figure 5.22
Three cheers for the red, white, and orange.

Figure 5.21
Righty lighty.

Got one layer left? Be practical and make this one a basic black-and-white, for creating dark accents later in the project. **Surface Control > Express Texture**, with the settings shown in Figure 5.23, will give you the high-contrast image in Figure 5.24.

94

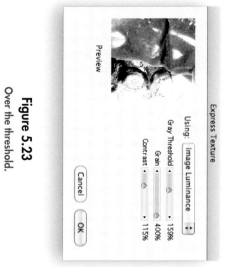

Figure 5.23
Over the threshold.

Many Paths to Lightenment

You can get the same results using two effects in the **Tonal Control** menu: **Adjust Colors**, where you'll reduce **Saturation** to zero, followed by a **Brightness/Contrast** adjustment. But using **Express Texture** gets you a lot more style points.

Figure 5.24
Basic black and white.

Your **Layers** panel should look similar to the one in Figure 5.25. Notice the layers have been named for easy reference and to remind you how each effect was created. All of that was just preparation, like cutting the vegetables before you really start cooking.

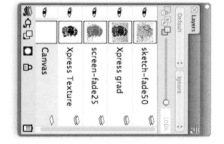

Figure 5.25
Ready for cooking.

Freestyle Cloning

The cloned painting of Betsy you saw at the beginning of this project can be created with any version of Painter. It doesn't require using the new **Clone Source** panel in Painter 12. Use **File > Quick Clone** to get a blank canvas that automatically has the layered image as its clone source. In order to get clone color from a particular layer, just highlight the desired layer and turn off the visibility of any layers above it. Tracing paper is available, as usual. Toggle it on and off frequently with the keyboard shortcut **Cmd/Ctrl+T**, so you can see your progress.

There isn't a custom palette for what follows, but you can easily make your own from this list of the variants I used:

- Soft Cloner
- Fiber Cloner
- Pointed Stump Blender
- Flat Oil Cloner
- Colored Pencil Cloner
- Watercolor Fine Cloner

Custom Brush Icons

A custom palette with five variants from the same Brush category could be confusing. Create your own icons for them in Painter 12. Use the ones I provided, shown in Figure 5.26, or make your own. Drag a rectangular selection around the "fiber" swatch, and then right-click (**Ctrl+click** on the Mac) **Fiber Cloner** in your custom palette. A pop-up menu appears, allowing you to choose **Capture Custom Icon**. Your selection will replace the little rubber stamp for that variant. If you choose **Set Custom Icon**, you can browse for any image on your drive. Figure 5.27 shows all the new icons in place. When your stylus hovers over one, you'll see the color version and a tooltip.

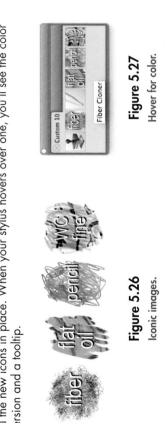

Figure 5.26
Iconic images.

Figure 5.27
Hover for color.

Meanwhile, back at the canvas…. Use the Soft Cloner to paint the face exactly as it is in the three-tone screen layer. Switch to the **Xpress Grad** layer and scribble in the hair and bits of the blue wall with **Fiber Cloner** strokes. The tighter your scribbles, the curlier the hair! This stage is shown in Figure 5.28.

Smooth out most of the curls with the **Pointed Stump**. (You'll bring them back soon.) Add a few scribbles with the **Flat Oil Cloner**, to get the feel of it. This stage is shown in Figure 5.29.

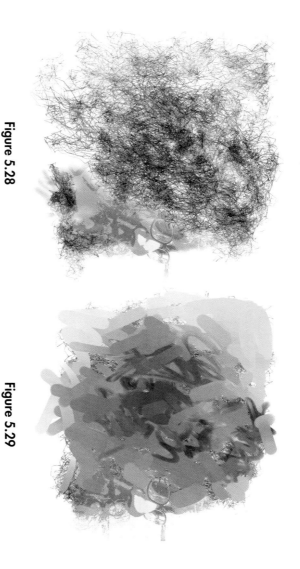

Figure 5.28
Kinky!

Figure 5.29
Relax, a little.

Scribble the curls back in with the **Fiber Cloner**. Now these strokes are being applied over a colorful background with no white spaces showing. Develop the face by switching to the black-and-white layer and sketching in some of the darker bits with the **Colored Pencil Cloner**. Figure 5.30 shows my results.

Let yourself go and add lots more curly hair with a combination of **Flat Oil** and **Colored Pencil Cloner** strokes. Fill in more of the blue wall with **Flat Oil Cloner** and **Pointed Stump** blending. For the shirt collar, switch to the three-tone screen layer. The image in Figure 5.31 also includes some strokes on Betsy's face using the colorful **Xpress Grad** layer.

Figure 5.30
Dark shadows.

Figure 5.31
Who does your hair?

For finishing touches use the **Sketch-Fade** layer, with the textured pale yellow wall. When you clone from this wall, allow bits of blue to show through. Finally, use the **Watercolor Fine Cloner** to paint the stripes on Betsy's shirt. You've produced a playful portrait purely with pixels, but based on a traditional painting.

Funny Features

Forty years of creating caricatures at events has allowed me to develop some skill at observing facial characteristics—and messing with them, on both traditional paper and digital canvas. Here's your chance to try your hand at facial distortion. Open **Jan.jpg** from the **People > Heads** folder (unless you prefer fooling around with someone you know). Jan's head shot appears alongside my humorous version in Figure 5.32. Your goal is to capture the essence of the face and its expression, by simplifying and exaggerating its elements.

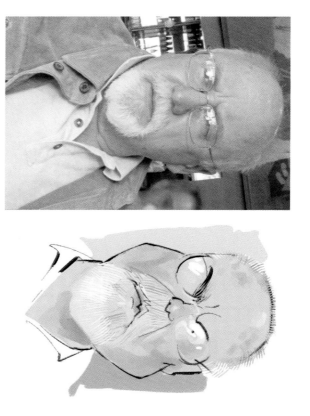

Figure 5.32

Jan, the man and the 'toon.

My favorite Painter variants for creating caricature, either live or in my studio, are:

■ Dry Ink

■ Chunky Oil Pastel

■ Pointed Stump

■ Scratchboard Rake

■ Cover Pencil

The **Dry Ink** variant of the **Pens** category is great for outlines. This brush makes a bristly line with wide variations in thickness as a function of stylus pressure. It's always 100% opaque and does not show paper grain. The first stages in Jan's caricature, shown in Figure 5.33, were done with **Dry Ink**. I changed the shape of his head and gave him a stronger neck. I really like his scowl, and plan to make the most of it.

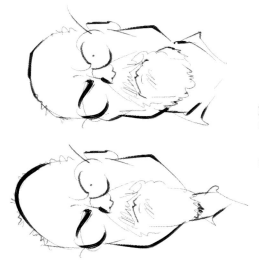

Figure 5.33
Neck and neck.

Life Is Short—Don't Erase!

That is my motto, and there is no eraser in the list. However, you can easily remove unwanted pixels by switching to white and painting out large areas with either **Dry Ink** or **Oil Pastel**. For tiny corrections, use the **Cover Pencil**. The word "Cover" in its name means that it is capable of covering dark pixels with lighter colors.

Add a new layer for color, using **Gel** or **Multiply** method, so the outlines will show through. Create a new color set for the flesh tones and shadows. Make a rectangular selection around Jan's nose, and use the **New Color Set from Selection** command in the **Color Set** pop-up menu. Figure 5.34 shows the selection and the color set derived from it.

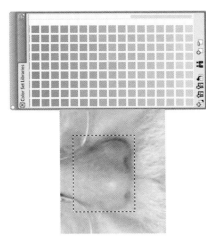

Figure 5.34
Nasal colors.

Fill in skin tones with the **Dry Ink** brush and dab on blocky strokes of rosy tints or shadow colors with the **Oil Pastel**. Then blend the edges of colors with the **Pointed Stump**. Adding a green tint enhances reflection on the glasses. Only one eye is needed (simplify!) and a tiny dot will do. The beard and what remains of Jan's hair are done with the **Scratchboard Rake**, a timesaving brush for applying several parallel lines at once. My rake strokes are enhanced with **Color Variability** settings that allow each stroke to contain lines that vary by **Hue**, **Saturation**, and/or **Value** (brightness). Find **Color Variability** controls grouped with **Brush Control** panels in Painter 12, or with the **Color** palettes in earlier versions. Figure 5.35 shows colors blended and rake strokes added.

For the finished art, I eliminated some of the black lines and changed the shape of Jan's jaw one more time.

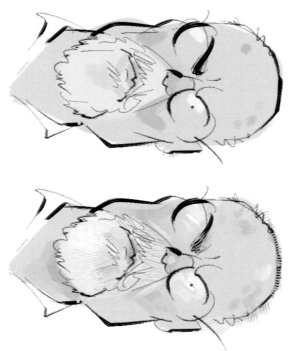

Figure 5.35
Getting more rakish.

What's Next?

You have completed the basic lessons in digital painting, and learned a few advanced techniques! There are many more Painter brushes and features to explore in the lessons to follow. You may already have some favorite Painter tools. Are you developing a style of your own? Consider working in a variety of styles, and choosing among them when you begin a new project.

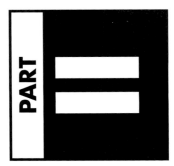

Beyond
the Basics

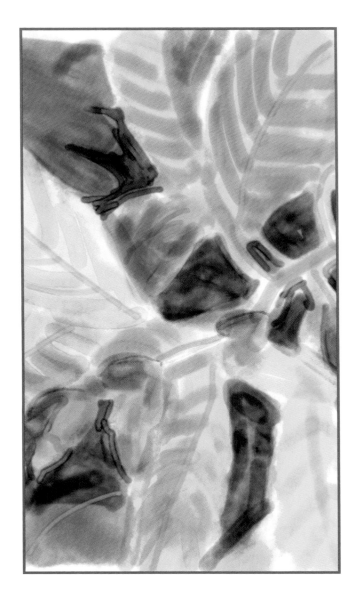

Customize Me!

This lesson is devoted to helping you create the kind of Painter environment you want, from the way the desktop workspace looks to the icons for your brushes. You will also examine more of the variables that influence brush behavior, so you can tweak them to perform exactly as you want. I saved this discussion for the middle of the book because I wanted to let you ride around in this amazing sports car for a while before I make you get out to look under the hood.

You've already been customizing some features that were included in art projects, like grouping brushes into custom palettes and setting the sensitivity of pressure with **Brush Tracking**. Chances are you've been learning about some other features just by poking around. Let's poke around together.

What's Your Preference?

Setting preferences is the first step in managing Painter's behavior. The default settings are optimized for most situations, but by now you know some of the options you prefer. I'm inclined to accept the factory settings for **General Preferences**. I'm inclined to accept the shown in Figure 6.1, is another story.

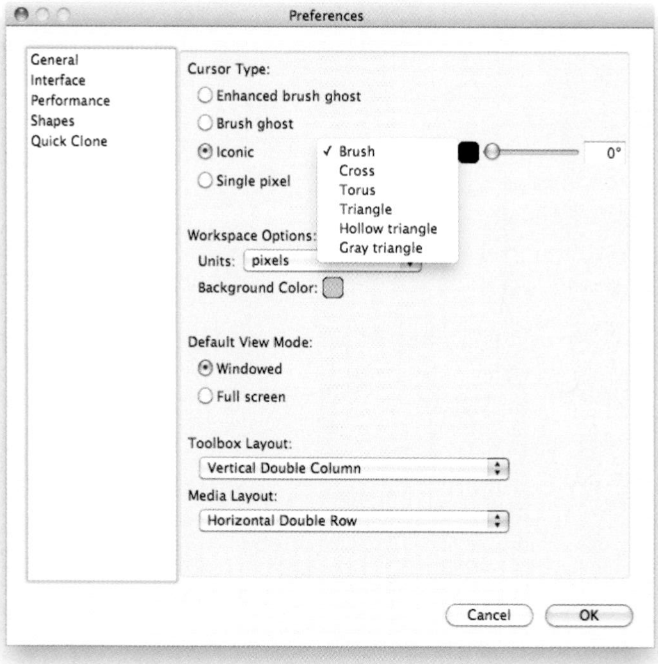

Figure 6.1
Interface time.

Choice of the **Cursor Type** is an important decision, because you'll be looking at it constantly while you draw and paint. If you choose an iconic cursor you can determine its angle, unless it's the torus (science-talk for donut). My preference is for **Brush ghost**, an outline of the current brush tip. This gives me information about the size and shape of the brush I'm using. A single pixel is precise but too hard to see, especially at my age. **Enhanced brush ghost** shows you the angle of your Wacom stylus, in case you really don't know, but it's a memory hog.

Workspace Units are pixels by default, and it's a good idea to get used to that. I'm finally giving up relying on inches. (But I still do insist that my temperature be taken in Fahrenheit.) For **View mode**, choose **Windowed** if you want easy access to everything else on your desktop, or **Full Screen** to eliminate distractions. **Toolbox Layout** can be vertical or horizontal, arranged as a double or single column. I like a vertical double column, so I can see all the Tools at a glance, same as I use for Photoshop. **Media Layout** refers to libraries of **Gradients**, **Patterns**, **Nozzles**, **Looks**, and **Weaves**. **Paper** has been promoted to a space on the actual **Toolbox**.

Moving on to the **Performance** section, do what you can to optimize for speed and efficiency. If you have a secondary drive or partition, use it for the **Scratch Drive**. Reduce the **Undo Levels** from the default of 32. Why in my day we only had one Undo—and we liked it! I suggest you uncheck the two **View** options in the **Performance** section.

The **Shapes** section deals with Painter's **Bezier Curve** or vector features. This is where you manage **Fills** and **Stokes**, **Anchor Points**, **Handles**, and **Wings**. Painter **Preferences** has a new section assigned to **Quick Clone** options. By default all boxes are checked. My preferences are shown in Figure 6.2. I often use **Quick Clone** to simply trace a photo, and I don't need the **Cloner Brushes** for that. I prefer to keep the **Clone Source** image open in any case.

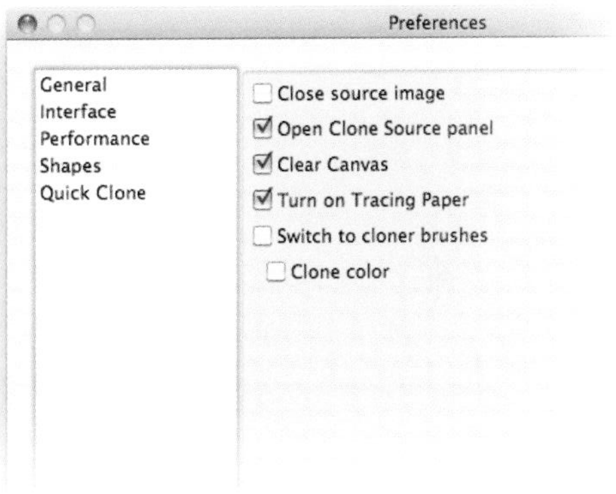

Figure 6.2
Open source.

Clone Outsourcing

Painter 12 allows you to choose (via the new **Clone Source** panel) any image on your hard drive to function as a clone source, whether it's open or not.

Brush Tracking, shown in Figure 6.3, is found in the **Preferences** menu, and is an essential tool for customizing any brush variant to your touch—the pressure and speed of your stroke. Painter 12 will actually remember the setting for individual brush variants! Access **Brush Tracking** anytime with a handy keyboard shortcut: **Shift+Cmd/Ctrl+, (comma)**. I found that shortcut while I looked at the last item in the **Preferences** menu: **Customize Keys**. This section has a list of all existing shortcuts for reference and lets you specify custom keys for any menu item.

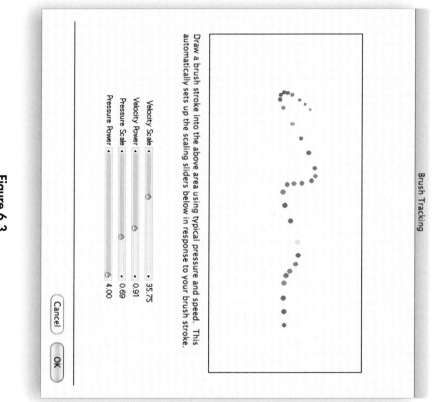

Brush Tracking

Draw a brush stroke into the above area using typical pressure and speed. This automatically sets up the scaling sliders below in response to your brush stroke.

Velocity Scale	35.75
Velocity Power	0.91
Pressure Scale	0.69
Pressure Power	4.00

Cancel   OK

Figure 6.3
Don't forget the Shift+Cmd/Ctrl+, (comma) shortcut!

Pals and Libs

Pals is short for **Custom Palettes,** compact little groupings of brushes, media, and/or commands that you gather together for a specific project or technique. *Libs* refers to **Libraries,** which are collections of one kind of media content such as papers, patterns, and gradients.

Let's review the basics of making and managing **Custom Palettes.** Begin making a new custom palette by pressing the **Shift** key as you drag a brush variant away from the **Brush Selector**. Figure 6.4 shows the simplest possible custom palette, containing one item, as well as a more complex palette with more brush variants, two paper textures, a couple of gradients and a pattern, as well as menu commands. The papers were included with the **Shift**-drag maneuver, and the command was added using **Add Command** from the **Window > Custom Palette** menu. The **Add Command** dialog box, shown in Figure 6.5, prompts you to choose a command and then add it to any open custom palette or start a new palette. The size and shape of the box holding your palette items can be changed by dragging edges or corners in or out. Contents can be **Shifted** around or eliminated by **Shift**-dragging them out of the box.

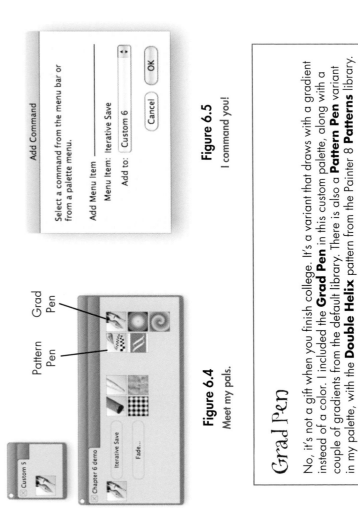

Figure 6.4
Meet my pals.

Pattern Pen   Grad Pen

Figure 6.5
I command you!

Add Command

Select a command from the menu bar or from a palette menu.

Add Menu Item

Menu Item: Iterative Save

Add to: Custom 6

Cancel   OK

Grad Pen

No, it's not a gift when you finish college. It's a variant that draws with a gradient instead of a color. I included the **Grad Pen** in this custom palette, along with a couple of gradients from the default library. There is also a **Pattern Pen** variant in my palette, with the **Double Helix** pattern from the Painter 8 **Patterns** library.

Use the **Custom Palette Organizer**, shown in Figure 6.6, to give your palettes descriptive names and to delete any unwanted palettes. The **Import** button allows you to load a custom palette that's not already on your desktop, including those that I've provided for you on the website that supports this book. The **Export** option lets you save any highlighted palette with a PAL file extension.

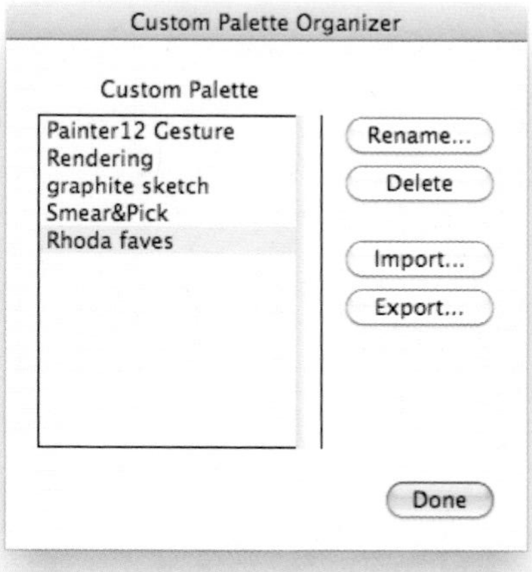

Figure 6.6
Let's get organized.

Iconography

Although the two **Pen** variants in the sample palette have the same icon (because they belong to the same category) they are easy to tell apart because of their positions. The placement of **Gradients** next to the **Grad Pen** also serves as a clue. Suppose you want three or more items from the same category in a custom palette. Painter 12 makes it easy to change from the category icon to any other image or simply to the name of the variant. Figure 6.7 shows the choices you get when you right-click (**Ctrl**-click) the icon. **Capture Custom Icon** is available only if you have already made a selection in the current image. A colorful mark was made with the **Grad Pen** and then selected. The resulting icon below it will have the same colors when your stylus hovers over it. **View as Text** replaces the icon with the name of the variant, which can then be changed using the **Rename** command.

Figure 6.7
Icon changes.

Icon Swaps

In Lesson 4, "The Great 'scape," you used a custom palette composed entirely of **Airbrush** variants and in Lesson 5, "Be a People Person," there is a project using mostly **Cloner** variants. Take another look at how those icons were customized.

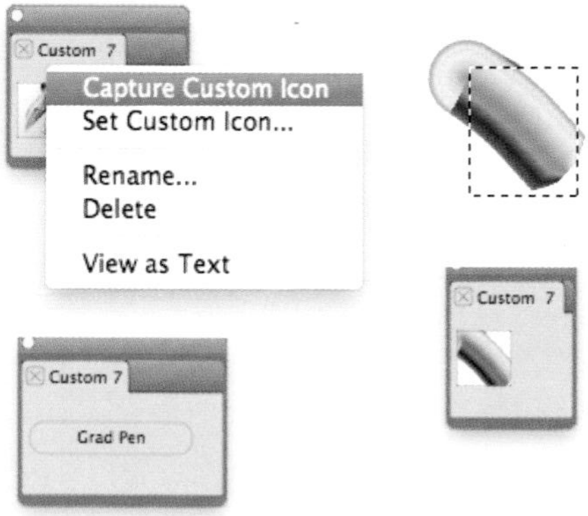

Movers and Removers

Previous versions of Painter allowed for **Papers** and **Media** libraries to be customized with a Mover utility. It's even easier in Painter 12 to make your own libraries—just drag and drop items from one collection to another. If you want to copy an item, press the **Option/Alt** key as you drag. Figure 6.8 shows other tools for managing papers. **New Library** opens a blank container that you can drag items into and then **Export** (save) with a descriptive name. **Import** allows you to **Load** other libraries from anywhere on your hard drive. **Capture Paper** is available when you have an active selection in your current image. It makes a repeating grayscale tile of the selection and adds it to the current Paper library. Some of these commands are also available in the pop-up menu, where you'll find **Paper Library View** options for swatch size. You can choose to view swatches as a list, with their names alongside each tiny thumbnail, as shown in Figure 6.9.

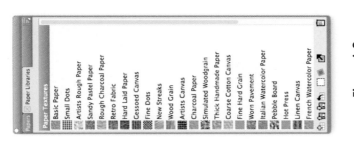

Figure 6.9

Show us your list.

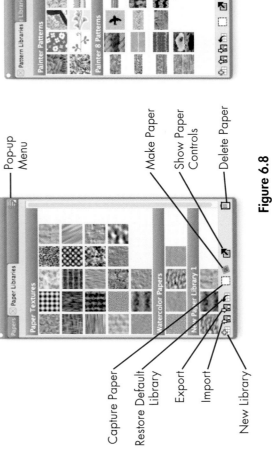

Figure 6.8

Your Library card never expires.

Pop-up Menu

Make Paper

Show Paper Controls

Delete Paper

Capture Paper

Restore Default Library

Export

Import

New Library

Media Makers

Not only can you group existing Papers and Media content any way you want, but you can make your own original papers, patterns, gradients, and other content. For a brief tutorial on capturing paper textures, see the section, "Papers Please," in Lesson 3 associated with Figures 3.15 through 3.19.

Here's a quick lesson on making a pattern from scratch. Make one of the three pearls shown in Figure 6.10 by painting a circular selection with the **Digital Airbrush** and **Detail Airbrush** using shades of pink. Use **Edit > Copy (Cmd/Ctrl+C)** and **Edit > Paste (Cmd/Ctrl+V)** to make another layer for a second pearl. Apply **Effects > Tonal Control > Adjust Colors** and move the **Hue Shift** slider, shown in Figure 6.11, to the left until you get a lavender shade. Repeat those steps to get the third pearl, then line them up for a tight rectangular selection. Use the **Capture Pattern** settings shown, and the new **Pattern** will take its place in the current Library. Test the pattern by painting a beaded stroke with **Pattern Pen Masked**.

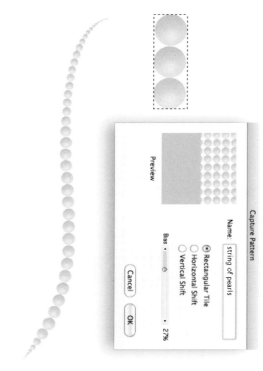

Figure 6.10
String beads.

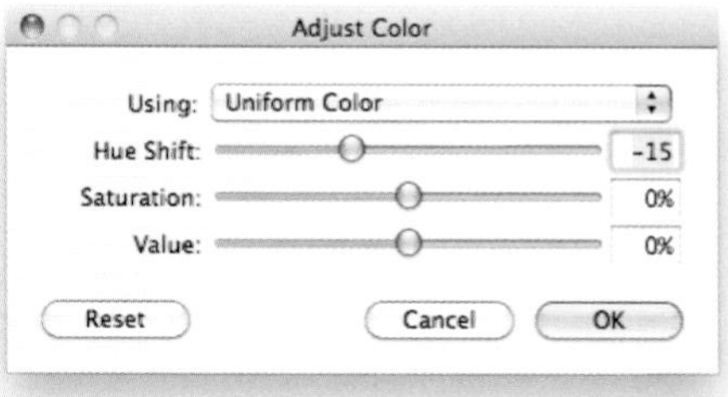

Figure 6.11
Color shift.

Some of the items in the default **Gradient Libraries**, shown in Figure 6.12, are **Spiral** style, others are **Circular**, **Radial**, or **Linear** at various angles. With the **Gradient Control** panel open you can switch any gradient to another style, as well as choose a single or double configuration and its direction. The example shows the **Aquatic Neon Gradient** changed from a **Spiral** to a double **Radial** style.

You can customize the colors and the way they blend by using the **Edit Gradient** controls. Make some changes to **Emerald Dawn**, whose default color ramp is shown in Figure 6.13. Delete some of the **Color** control points for a smoother blend or to eliminate some colors by simply clicking on the control point and pressing **Delete/Backspace**. Add a new color by clicking the place inside the **Color** ramp bar where you want it to appear. A new **Color** control point will appear. Assign a color to it as you would choose a color for painting, by choosing from the **Color** panel. I added a turquoise blue near the center of the ramp to get the results shown in Figure 6.14.

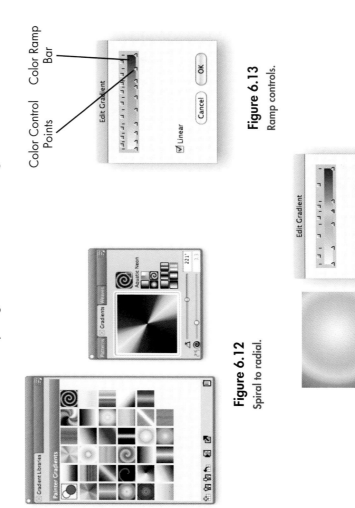

Figure 6.12
Spiral to radial.

Color Control   Color Ramp
Points   Bar

Figure 6.13
Ramp controls.

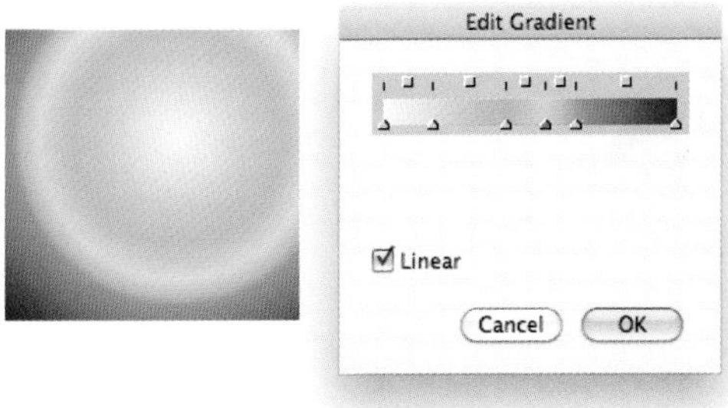

Figure 6.14
A new dawn.

Gimme Some Space

You've seen what a time-saver it is to have a custom palette for every situation. You can also open and arrange all the panels and tools you'll need for a given project and save the whole layout as a workspace. Get a feel for how some Painter masters have used this capability by importing some of their workspaces. Then create your own based on an existing workspace, or start one from scratch.

Make Arrangements

A **New Workspace** can take a while to load. It's quicker to save a palette layout using **Arrange Palettes > Save Layout.**

Brush Controls

There are 26 panels in the **Brush Controls** section of the **Window** menu. You might never need most of them, but it's good to know where they are.

Help!

I cover just a fraction of the vast number of **Brush Controls.** Complete details on this topic and anything else you want to know about Painter 12 are available at your fingertips. Just click on **Help** at the top of your screen. Use the **Index** under **Corel Painter 12 Help** to go directly to a specific item of interest, or explore the other features that provide insights into the program.

Choose **Square Hard Pastel** and make a few strokes. Open the **General** and **Dab Profile** panels from **Brush Controls**, as shown in Figure 6.15. The **Dab Type** is **Captured**, and is a small image that looks like a rectangular sponge. The **Method** is **Cover**, meaning that light colors can cover up darker ones, as shown at the top of Figure 6.16. The **Subcategory** is **Grainy Hard Cover,** and you can create a different look by changing it. The middle stroke in Figure 6.16 was made with **Grainy Edge Flat Cover**, and the bottom stroke uses **Grainy Soft Cover.** The term *grainy* means responsive to Paper texture, so these strokes will look different if you switch to another paper. Those little squares to the right of the **Dab Preview** indicate various ways color can be distributed across a stroke. Be sure to click the **Reset Tool** icon after you finish fiddling with this variant, to restore its default settings.

Figure 6.16

Three kinds of grainy.

Figure 6.15

Basic controls.

Just a Dab

The most significant variable that determines the "personality" of a brush is its **Dab Type**. Figure 6.17 shows them all. Most items on this list are clearly descriptive, although some are a bit more esoteric. The **Airbrush** category, for example, has some variants that use the **Airbrush** dab type, but others use **Circular** or **Computed Circular** dabs. Get into the habit of looking at the **Dab Type** and **Dab Profile** every time you use an unfamiliar brush.

Figure 6.17

Dab Types galore.

Switch to the **Wet Acrylic** variant and notice that its **Dab Type** is **Static Bristle**. The **Dab Profile** shown in Figure 6.18 shows numerous bristles, as you would expect. Open the **Static Bristle** control panel, also shown. Experiment with changes in the **Thickness, Clumpiness,** and other sliders. Can you predict how changes will affect the stroke? Figure 6.19 shows how settings influence the look of a bristle brush.

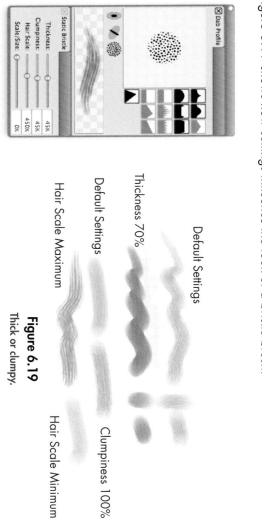

Figure 6.18
A bristly dab.

Default Settings

Thickness 70%

Default Settings

Hair Scale Maximum

Clumpiness 100%

Hair Scale Minimum

Figure 6.19
Thick or clumpy.

Custom Brushes

Suppose you want to have your thicker or clumpier **Wet Acrylic** brush available permanently, so you don't have to change the default settings next time. You can make a new variant using **Brushes > Save Variant**. Give it a distinctive name such as **Clumpy Wet Acrylic**. Or you can choose to apply the changes to the original **Wet Acrylic** by using the **Brushes > Set Default Variant** command. If you go to the trouble of creating just the right combination of qualities for a special brush, it's a very good idea to preserve it.

After you have several custom brush variants, consider making a special library for them. You can make a new library for any combination of existing brushes. If you only want a few brush categories for a project, or there are some categories you never use, make a custom library with only the items you want. Smaller brush libraries are more efficient in terms of RAM use.

To make a new brush library, start by creating a new folder within the **Painter 12 > Brushes** folder on your hard drive. Then systematically make and name a new folder for each category, and copy/paste the XML files for all of the variants you want to include in their proper places. Relaunch Painter to access your new library from the **Library** list in the **Brushes** pop-up menu. Don't forget to copy/paste the JPEGs needed to make the icons.

Drag 'n' Drop

If you want a new brush library that simply has fewer categories and variants, it might be quicker to copy entire categories into your new library folder and delete the variants you don't want. Be sure to use the **Option/Alt** key as you drag, so that you leave the original items in the default library.

A Stitch in Time

Here's a real life challenge in creating a custom brush for a special project. I recently finished an illustration assignment for a how-to book on quilting. It required nearly 200 drawings showing the stages in creating quilt projects, from cutting fabric to sewing the pieces together. I realized it would save me a lot of time if I could make a **Pen** variant composed of a broken line that looked like machine stitching. I did it, and you can, too.

Open the **Size**, **Spacing**, and **Angle** panels in the **Brush Controls** list, along with **General** and **Dab Profile** panels already open. You can dismiss the **Bristle** controls. You'll develop a stitching pen from the **Broad Smooth Pen**, which already has most of the qualities you need, such as the **Circular Dab** type, **Cover** method, and a non-grainy subcategory. The **Dab Profile** for this variant is shown in Figure 6.20. The dab is already squeezed into an oval. You'll need to reduce the size, increase the space between dabs, and get the stitches at the correct angle. As you try each change, make practice strokes on a canvas as well as observe the **Stroke Preview**. My "scratch pad" appears in Figure 6.21.

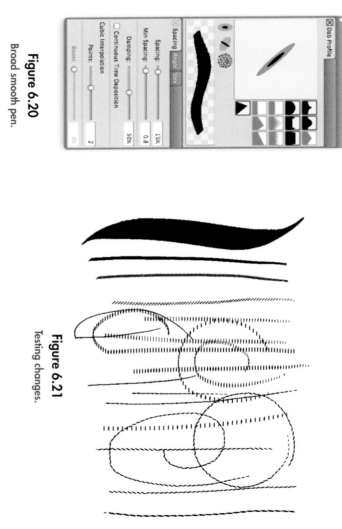

Figure 6.20
Broad smooth pen.

Figure 6.21
Testing changes.

Start by moving the top slider in the **Size** panel from 40 pixels to about 6. You don't want any variation in the size of the stitches, so choose **None** in the **Expression** field, instead of the default **Pressure**. Now the setting for **Minimum Size** won't matter. Test to see that your settings result in a much smaller brush whose stroke does not vary in width.

Now turn your attention to the **Spacing** panel and move the top slider all the way to the maximum on the right. That's not enough space between dabs, so move the **Min Spacing** slider to the maximum as well. Those changes can be seen in Figure 6.22.

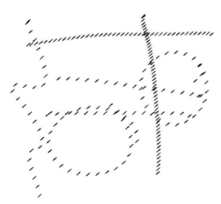

Figure 6.22
Getting spaced out.

Time to work with the **Angle** panel, shown in Figure 6.23, along with the updated **Dab Profile**. A **Squeeze** of 26% seems about right—100% is a perfect circle. The angle needs to make each "stitch" follow the line of the stroke, in whatever direction the stroke is made. The settings shown in Figure 6.24 will do the trick. The angle of 176 degrees shows what you want in the **Stroke Preview**. **Expression** of the angle must be **Direction**, and finally you need to have all possible angles available by setting **Ang Range** to the maximum (360 degrees).

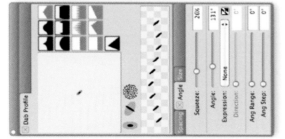

Figure 6.23
Wrangle the angle.

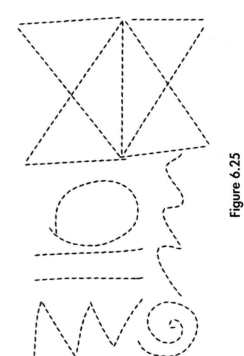

Figure 6.24
Expression and Range set.

With the **Angles** handled, you can see if **Size** or **Spacing** needs any tweaking. The test strokes in Figure 6.25 show everything working to perfection, with the new variant ready to save. The strokes at the right were made in Painter's **Straight Line Strokes** mode, which you'll find next to the default **Freehand Strokes** icon in the **Property Bar**.

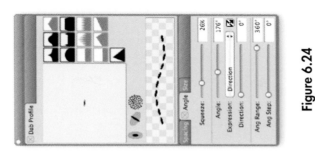

Figure 6.25
In stitches.

Check Your Oils

Variants in the same category can have a variety of **Dab Types.** Figure 6.26 shows squiggles made with seven brushes in the **Oil** group, each with a different **Dab Type.** To experiment with these variants, make a custom palette as shown in Figure 6.27. Replace each identical icon with the name of the brush, by choosing **View as Text** after you right-click (**Ctrl**-click) the icon.

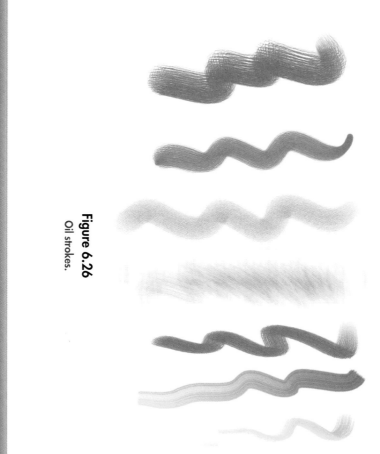

Figure 6.26
Oil strokes.

Figure 6.27
Custom oil palette.

What makes the two variants on the right run out of paint? Choose **Real Oils Short** and notice that the setting for **Blend** in the **Property Bar** is 55%. The tooltip for **Blend**, which will appear when your cursor is on that item, tells you that **Blend**, "affects how oil is mixed between colors." In this case the color is the white background. What will happen when you make a stroke across several other colors? Use the **Paint Bucket** to fill a rectangle with a colorful gradient, and then make several strokes with **Real Oils Short**. I used the same Magenta color as before, and the results are shown in Figure 6.28. The brush still runs out of paint, but it takes other colors along with it.

Figure 6.28
Mix and blend.

Switch to the **Oily Bristle** brush. This variant has a 40% **Blend** amount, so you can expect it to mix with other colors, but not as much as **Real Oils Short**. There are two additional variables in the **Property Bar** to examine—**Viscosity** and **Wetness.** Move the **Viscosity** slider up or down and test the results. Figure 6.29 shows, from left to right, the default **Viscosity** setting of 25%, 0%, and 100%. At the minimum setting, paint never runs out, and at the maximum, it runs out much quicker. Now I'm wondering what makes the color less saturated as the stroke gets longer.

Figure 6.29
Viscous cycles.

Detective Work

Descriptions about brush controls in the online **Help** section are useful, but it's more effective (and more fun) to investigate on your own by changing settings and testing the results.

Look at the **Wetness** amount, and once again see what happens when you try extreme settings. Figure 6.30 shows the difference between a default stroke on the left, and a stroke with **Wetness** reduced to zero. I seem to have stumbled on a way to retain the purity of color (saturation) throughout the stroke!

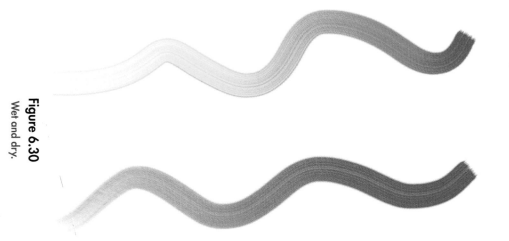

Figure 6.30
Wet and dry.

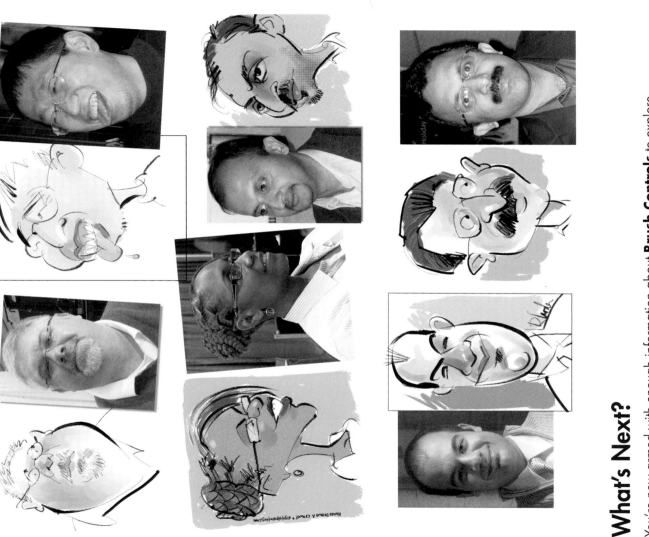

What's Next?

You're now armed with enough information about **Brush Controls** to explore more of them with confidence. You'll have plenty of chances to work with that knowledge elsewhere in the book. In the next lesson, you'll learn all about Painter's **Text** tool, and how to do tricks with type. There is also a "quilt" project, inspired by the illustration that led to creating the sewing machine stitch brush.

7 Getting Graphic

Graphic designers typically use a vector-based program like Illustrator or a page-layout program such as InDesign to create the text needed to accompany an illustration. (It's good to own stock in Adobe Systems.) But if a special effect is desired for a few words or letters, it might be best to use a pixel-based program and create text as an image. Painter has a variety of terrific options for text effects.

Special effects aren't just for type. By the time you finish this lesson, you'll be able to paint with liquid metal, melted chocolate, flowers, and gravel. If that's not exciting enough, you will also get a chance to burn, blob, and marble.

For this lesson, you'll use the following items from the website that supports this book:

- Images: **Lattice_Leaves.jpg, Sashiko.jpg, cupcakes2.jpg, chocolate_icing1.jpg,** and **chocolate_icing2.jpg**

Just My Type

Painter's **Text** tool icon is a capital letter **T**. When it is active, the **Property Bar** gives you many of the standard choices for font, point size, and alignment. You can choose to have a drop shadow or an interior shadow applied automatically as you enter text. There are separate color and opacity controls as well as composite method choices for how the text and its shadow will interact with layers below them. Just highlight **Text Attributes** or **Shadow Attributes** to alter them independently. Figure 7.1 gets you acquainted with these options. When you click on your canvas with the Text tool, a special layer is automatically created, with the **T** symbol showing that this is editable type. The first few words you type appear in the layer panel.

The **Text** panel, shown in Figure 7.2, gives you most of the **Property Bar** choices and more. Here's where you'll adjust *tracking* (letter spacing), *leading* (the spacing between lines of text), and assign a curve style. Blur effects at the bottom of the palette can be assigned to the text and shadow independently. I applied a 12.3 blur to soften the shadow behind the pink letters.

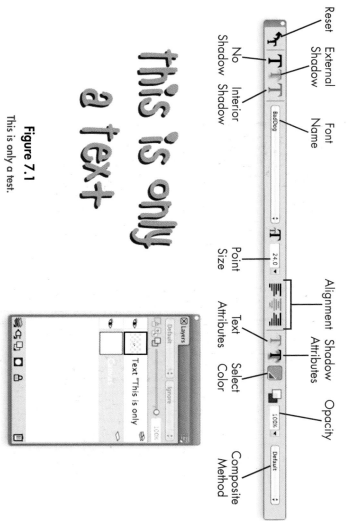

Reset
External Shadow
No Shadow
Interior Shadow
Font Name
Point Size
Alignment
Text Attributes
Shadow Attributes
Select Color
Opacity
Composite Method

BadDog
24.0
100%
Default

Figure 7.1
This is only a test.

Layers
Default
Ignore
Text "This is only
100%
Default

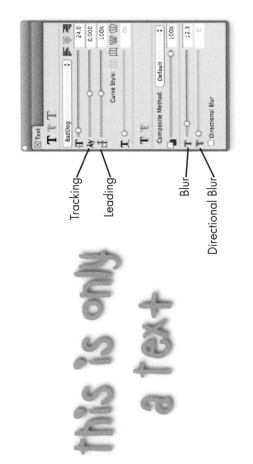

Tracking

Leading

Blur

Directional Blur

Figure 7.2

Leading rhymes with wedding.

The top sample in Figure 7.3 has text in blue with a magenta drop shadow. The other variations were made just by changing composite methods or adding a blur. The middle sample uses the **Reverse-Out** method. The bottom sample uses **Screen** method for the text and a 30 blur applied to the shadow.

Figure 7.3

Taken out of context.

126

Magazine Logo

Let's practice creative typography with an assignment to design the title of a magazine for quiltmakers called *Quilty Pleasures*. There is a blog and an unrelated website using that title, but no magazine yet. The plan is to find a typeface that is bold enough to be filled with the image of a quilt. Figure 7.4 shows two possible candidates.

Figure 7.4
Gimme a "Q".

The first sample is in a font called *Impact* and the second line is set in *Lithos Pro Black*. Both of these are bold *sans serif* fonts, but *Impact* is more *condensed*. Condensed means that the letters are quite a bit taller than they are wide, leaving very little white space. Figure 7.5 demonstrates the difference between *serif* and *sans serif* letters. *Serifs* are the extra little strokes that are used to finish off the top or bottom of a letter. *Sans* means "without," so a *sans serif* font has simpler, cleaner lines. Which of these samples are *bold* and which are *light*? Can you find the one that is most *condensed*? Two of them are leaning a bit to the right, called *italic* or *oblique* style.

Figure 7.5
I shot the serif.

fonts of Wisdom

It's unlikely you'll have all the same fonts on your hard drive that are used in this project. Knowing how to describe the qualities of a typeface will help you find a substitute that is similar. Several font houses are included in the resources at the back of this book.

Figure 7.6
Nice bumping into you.

Got Fonts?

I chose *Lithos Pro Black* because I like the rounder shape of the "Q" and the all-caps letters that are nearly the same width. That looks a lot friendlier than *Impact*, better for a quilters 'zine. I changed the text color to black, in preparation for an effect coming later. To reduce the white space between letters, I moved the tracking slider in the **Text** panel a bit to the left, to –0.037. The result is an awkward bumping of the last two letters, as shown in Figure 7.6. The "Y" needs some retouching. I'll use a smooth **Pen** variant to trim away the excess pixels with white and fill in the black.

Rasterize Me!

As soon as you try to paint on a **Text** layer, a dialog box appears, asking if you want to commit the text to an image layer. Click the **Commit** button and you're good to go. You have just *rasterized* the text, transforming it into pixels. Look at the icon on your **Layers** panel to see the "T" is now gone. At this point the letters are no longer editable as text.

Figure 7.7 shows progress as I blend the **T** and **Y** characters together. I tilted the canvas to have better control and comfort, using the **Rotate Page** tool, which now has it's own apartment! Prior to version 12, it had to share a place in the **Toolbox** with the (ugh!) **Grabber**. You can restore the page to vertical by double-clicking on it when the **Rotate Page** tool is active or double-clicking the tool itself.

Figure 7.7
Two letters tied together form a *ligature*.

The image you'll use to fill the type is **Lattice_Leaves.jpg**, a gorgeous creation by Joy-Lily, a San Francisco quilt maven and silk painter. You'll find it in the **Things > Fabric & Textures** folder on the website that supports this book. **Copy (Cmd/Ctrl+C)** and **Paste (Cmd/Ctrl+V)** it on the black text document. Yes, it covers up the letters, but there is a **Composite** method that will replace all the black pixels with the quilt image, while leaving the white pixels of the background untouched. It is (wait for it) **Lighten** method! The quilt is lighter than black and the background is lighter than the quilt. Drag the quilt layer around with the **Layer Adjuster** tool until you are satisfied with the effect, as shown in Figure 7.8.

Figure 7.8
Joy-Lily quilt covers black text.

The quilt will look *quiltier* if you could see the top-stitching, a decorative pattern of stitches added after sewing all the pieces together. At the risk of gilding the Joy-Lily, you'll add top-stitching as a surface texture. The first step is to make a custom paper from an image of *Sashiko* patterns, ornamental Japanese stitching. Open **Sashiko.jpg**, a sampler of white stitching on a dark blue background. Make a rectangular selection around the pattern you want to use. I chose the leaf-circles at the bottom right, to stay in harmony with the leafy theme. Use **Effects > Tonal Control > Negative** to invert the colors. Now there is dark stitching against a light yellow background, shown in Figure 7.9. Drag a rectangular selection carefully to include just one complete element of the pattern. You're ready to make this "tile" into a paper texture. (Review the section on making custom paper in Lesson 3, "Have Another Layer," if needed.)

Figure 7.9
Invert your Sashiko.

Use the **Capture Paper** command in the **Paper Library** panel, shown in Figure 7.10, and give your new texture a name when prompted. *Sashiko Leaves* should do it. Your custom paper is now part of the current library. Figure 7.11 shows how the **Papers** panel looks when the new paper is chosen. Notice that the scale slider is set to 124%, which is ideal for the next step.

Figure 7.10
Capture your selection.

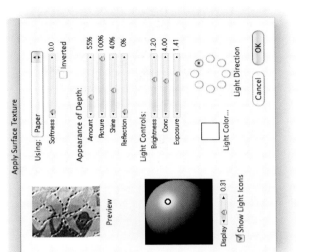

Figure 7.11
Choose your new paper.

Instead of painting the *Sashiko* texture onto the quilt with pastel strokes or any other grainy brush, you will use **Effects > Surface Control > Apply Surface Texture** to add all the stitching in an instant, complete with the illusion of depth! When you choose that command, the dialog box in Figure 7.12 appears. The most important setting is at the top, where you will specify your current paper as the source of tonal information. Use the settings shown or fiddle with them and observe changes in the **Preview** thumbnail. You can always use **Undo (Cmd/Ctrl+Z)** or **Edit > Fade** to reduce the effect by a percentage.

Figure 7.12
Change settings as needed.

129

Figure 7.13 has two variations, showing what a different effect you get if paper tonality is inverted (made negative). This can be achieved either by checking the invert box for the surface texture effect, or in the **Papers** panel. In one case, the stitches appear to be tiny dents in the surface, in the other they look like raised bumps. Yes, you could have saved a step and made the paper from the original white stitches on dark fabric.

Figure 7.13
Are you an inny or an outy?

What's Your Pleasure?

You still need to find a type style for the word "pleasure." For contrast, a casual script or other light-weight font should work nicely. Figure 7.14 shows, from the top, *Bronx, Imprint, Brush Script Italic,* and *Vivaldi Italic.*

If this were a real-world assignment you'd use two of them and let the client decide. Figure 7.15 shows the finished piece using *Brush Script Italic* in a peach color with a green drop shadow. This logo can be given a fresh look every month by changing the colors, even swapping in a different quilt photo.

Figure 7.14
Do I look fat in these fonts?

Figure 7.15
Ready, set, print.

More Text Tricks

What other stuff can you use to turn words into graphics? I thought you'd never ask. Let's take a tour of several techniques that can be used to produce stunning text effects.

Every version of Painter has a wonderful way to create marbling patterns. The basic method in traditional marbling requires a large shallow pan containing water. Drop blobs of oil-based or acrylic ink onto the surface of the water, creating a stone pattern. Drag a rake-like tool through the blobs in different directions until you are satisfied with the result. Carefully lay a piece of paper or fabric on the surface and lift it out. It has picked up the color. Digital marbling in Painter is done the same way, but you don't have to keep a mop handy for spills or wear a smock.

Type the word "Marbled" in a bold font, using any bright color. Pick a contrasting color in the Color panel for the next step, **Effects > Esoterica > Blobs**. The dialog box for **Blobs** is shown in Figure 7.16. It's important to designate **Current Color** for filling the blobs. Feel free to use other settings for number and size.

Figure 7.17 shows the result of applying blobs. The top sample has one set of blobs. To get results similar to the bottom sample, change color and repeat three or four more times. Use a 50% fade after some of the blobbing.

Figure 7.16
Prepare to blob.

Figure 7.17
The lava lamp look.

Effects > Esoterica > Apply Marbling will bring up the dialog box shown in Figure 7.18. You can either design your own formula for marbling or use the **Load** button in the **Rake Path** section to get the recipes provided. One right-to-left pull produces the image at the top of Figure 7.19. The **Bouquet** recipe automatically creates the marvelous effect at the bottom. A dark background was poured into the Canvas with the **Paint Bucket**.

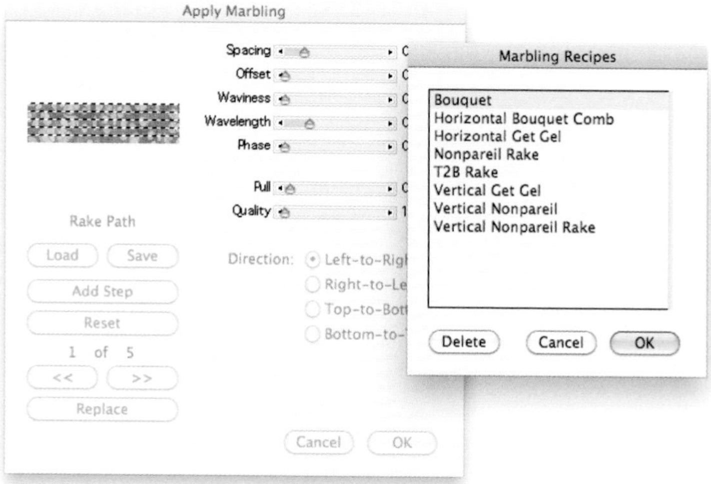

Figure 7.18
Which recipe makes marble cake?

Figure 7.19
You look marble-ous!

Wordless Marbling

You can, of course, use **Blobs** and **Apply Marbling** on a blank canvas. Try light colors and print the patterns on fine Japanese paper to create elegant stationery.

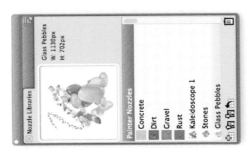

Figure 7.20
Pick your nozzle.

Let Us Spray

A feature that's been around since Painter was born is the **Image Hose**. This item has a slot in the **Brushes** panel with the icon of a garden hose pouring out tiny images. The variant list allows you to choose how the image bits are applied. **Linear** or **Spray** are the basic types, and you also get to choose how the size and angle of the image elements are determined. **P** (pressure), **D** (direction), and **R** (random) are most useful. So, **Linear-Size-P** means the image elements will pour out on a single line, with size being a function of stylus pressure. **Spray-Size-R Angle D** means the image bits will tumble out in a random array of sizes, but with their angles determined by the direction of your stroke. What comes out of the hose depends on which nozzle you choose from the **Nozzle Libraries** shown in Figure 7.20. It's one of the **Media Library** panels found under the **Window** menu.

Figure 7.21 shows a line of Glass Pebbles made with the **Linear-Size-P** variant, followed by Swallows applied with **Spray-Size-R**. I used a circular stroke with **Spray-Size-R Angle-D** to make the Red Poppies follow the direction of my circle. The direction will reverse depending on whether you draw clockwise or counter-clockwise. The bouquet of poppies was created with several concentric circular scribbles going clockwise.

Figure 7.21
Lines and sprays.

Some nozzles can be used for hand-written words that are self-descriptive. Spray a layer of **Concrete** down. Then use a linear variant when you switch your nozzle to **Dirt** and write the word out by hand. Finally, use the **Gravel** nozzle to finish the graphic in Figure 7.22.

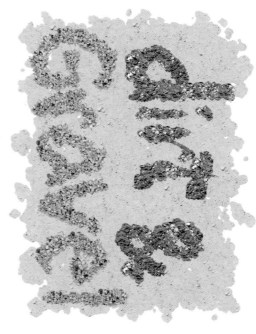

Figure 7.22
Quick and dirty signage.

Once More with Filling

Here's a way to make text look rusted and eroded. Type the word "rusty" in any suitable font with black for the text color. I'm using *Gill Sans Bold*. Make a new layer and switch **Composite Method** from **Default** to **Lighten**. Pick up the **Image Hose** and install the **Rust** nozzle. Spray the layer to completely cover the text but leave the white background unchanged. (Yes, this is the method that enabled you to fill the word "Quilty" with a photo.) This stage is shown in Figure 7.23.

Figure 7.23
My typing is a bit rusty.

Eroding the edges of the letters will require another effect. But first, you'll need to combine the rust and text layers, and make a new layer out of the result:

1. Use the **Drop** command in the **Layers** menu.

2. Click the **Magic Wand** tool on a white pixel to select them all.

3. Select **Invert Selection**, so only the rusty letters are active.

4. **Cut (Cmd/Ctrl+X)** and **Paste (Cmd/Ctrl+V)** to delete the rusty letters from the canvas and put them on a layer.

And now, welcome to the amazing **Dynamic** plug-ins! They are found at the bottom of the **Layers** panel (also in the **Layers** menu), and have an electric plug icon. Choose **Burn** and adjust settings in the dialog box, shown in Figure 7.24. Your settings will depend on the size and font you use, and how much erosion you desire.

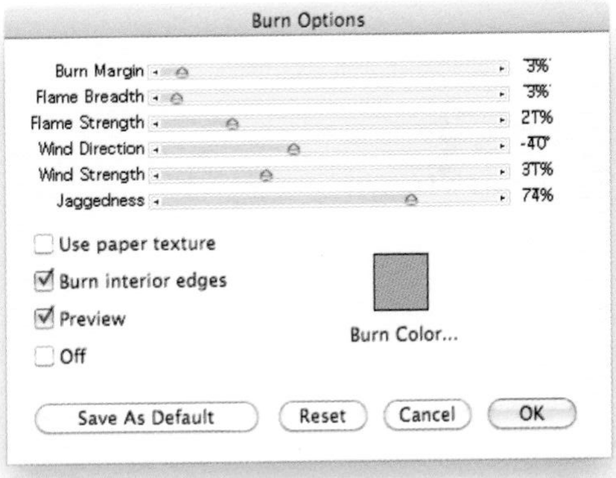

The final stage, shown in Figure 7.25, also has a drop shadow. This is made using a method quite different from creating an external shadow with the **Text** tool. **Effects > Objects > Create Drop Shadow** provides settings for offset, opacity, and a couple of other variables, but not color. Accept the default values and click OK. Figure 7.26 shows your **Layers** panel at this point, with the shadow on its own layer, grouped with the original layer. You can change its color now. Select only the Shadow layer, and turn on the **Preserve Transparency** function (it's blue when active). This will ensure that only the shadow pixels are changed.

Figure 7.24
Burn, baby, burn!

Figure 7.25
Distressed text.

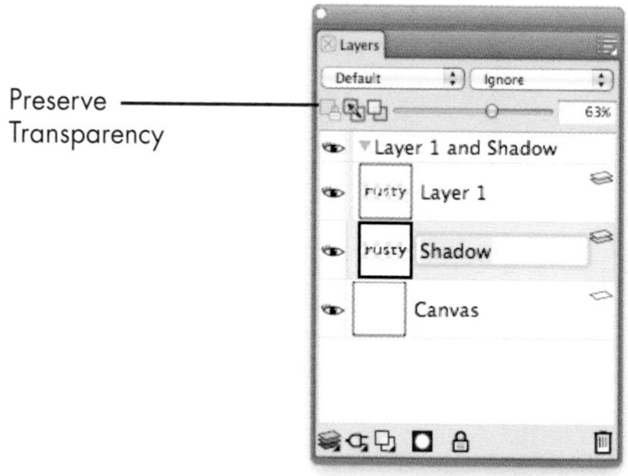

Preserve
Transparency

Figure 7.26
Me and my shadow.

Pick a dark reddish brown and pour color from the **Paint Bucket** tool. The shadow is now rusty, too. Handle with care, or you might need a tetanus shot.

The **Pattern Libraries** are shown in Figure 7.27, using the list view.

Pattern Recognition

Pattern Pens, a category whose icon is a checkered design coming out of a pen nib, provides completely different ways to paint with images.

Consider the Source

Patterns are a versatile source, literally. When you use a **Cloner** brush and have not assigned an image to be the **Clone Source**, the current pattern is the default source for color and value. When asked to decide what to use to fill a selection (or a blob), you can choose to use the current pattern.

Figure 7.27
Check them out at the library.

Compare pattern fills with pen strokes. A quick way to fill an area with the current pattern is to use the **Paint Bucket** tool, with **Source Image** chosen in the **Property Bar** for the fill. Just drag a rectangle on a blank canvas and it will be filled with the pattern. Use the **Pattern Pen Masked** variant to draw, write, or scribble with the same pattern. Figure 7.28 has fills and strokes made with *Thorny Rose Vines* and *Skein of Blue Yarn*. I reduced the size of the pen before writing "yarn." What is masked out of the pen stroke is the background color—black behind the thorny vines, for example.

Figure 7.28
Feeling thorny?

A Cocoa Logo

Make a fresh new canvas that will fit comfortably on your screen at 100% size, and visit the Dynamic plug-ins again. Choose **Liquid Metal** this time. Figure 7.29 shows the **Liquid Metal** controls, which must remain open while you work.

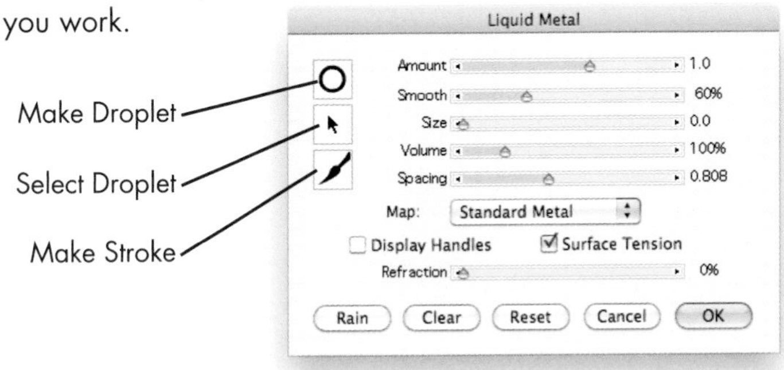

Make Droplet
Select Droplet
Make Stroke

Figure 7.29
Hot metal controls.

Practice making strokes with the brush, and switch to the circle to make metallic droplets. Notice the tendency for droplets to attract each other and run together! The **Undo** command won't work here, so if you want to remove a stroke or a droplet, use the arrow icon to select it and then press the **Delete/Backspace** key. Strokes are actually made up of a sequence of droplets. You can see them individually by enabling **Display Handles**. Figure 7.30 shows droplets and strokes and a detail with handles displayed.

The choice you make in the **Map** field determines the reflections on the strokes and drops. Changes will have a dramatic effect. Notice that **Clone Source** is one of the alternatives to the default **Standard Metal** in the list. You can specify any image, open or not, as a **Clone Source** using the **Clone Source** panel. With a little tweaking of the controls and preparing alternate source images for the reflection map, you can emulate a variety of liquids, including melted chocolate!

Figure 7.30
Show us your handles.

Source Recourse

If you're using an earlier versions of Painter, you'll need to open all images that will serve as a **Clone Source** and choose among them using **File > Clone Source.**

Use the **Clear** button to remove your practice strokes and drops. Make both of the chocolate icing images (from the **Things > Food** folder), shown in Figure 7.31, available as clone sources. Write "cocoa" with **Liquid Metal** strokes. I chose **chocolate_icing1.jpg** for my first effort, shown in Figure 7.32. Oops—I spelled the word incorrectly. No problem. I just use the arrow to drag droplets forming the unwanted letter down and drag the remaining letters over to fill the gap. I could have just deleted the extra droplets, but I like the messy look. In real life, you can simply eat your mistakes.

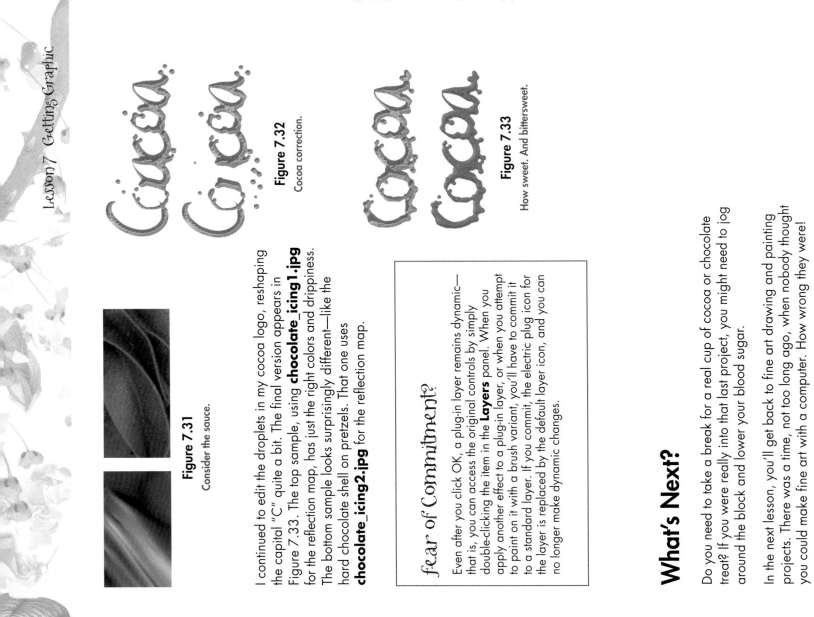

Figure 7.31
Consider the sauce.

Figure 7.32
Cocoa correction.

Figure 7.33
How sweet. And bittersweet.

I continued to edit the droplets in my cocoa logo, reshaping the capital "C" quite a bit. The final version appears in Figure 7.33. The top sample, using **chocolate_icing1.jpg** for the reflection map, has just the right colors and drippiness. The bottom sample looks surprisingly different—like the hard chocolate shell on pretzels. That one uses **chocolate_icing2.jpg** for the reflection map.

fear of Commitment?

Even after you click OK, a plug-in layer remains dynamic—that is, you can access the original controls by simply double-clicking the item in the **Layers** panel. When you apply another effect to a plug-in layer, or when you attempt to paint on it with a brush variant, you'll have to commit it to a standard layer. If you commit, the electric plug icon for the layer is replaced by the default layer icon, and you can no longer make dynamic changes.

What's Next?

Do you need to take a break for a real cup of cocoa or chocolate treat? If you were really into that last project, you might need to jog around the block and lower your blood sugar.

In the next lesson, you'll get back to fine art drawing and painting projects. There was a time, not too long ago, when nobody thought you could make fine art with a computer. How wrong they were!

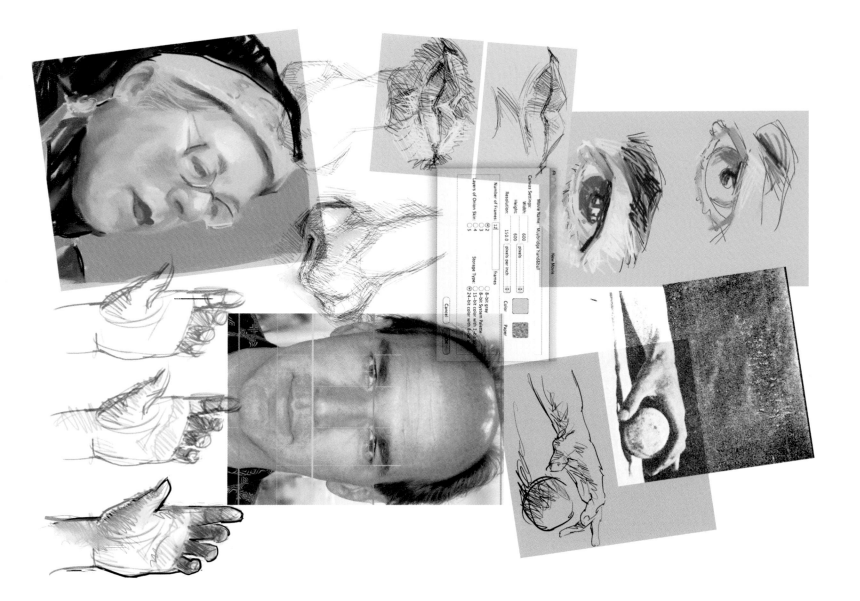

Drawn from Life

T raditional drawing classes often rely on studies of the human figure to teach the essentials of observing natural forms and transforming them into two-dimensional lines, shapes, and tones on paper or canvas. Mastery of the skills needed to draw the figure, head, and hands with correct proportions can take many years. This lesson will either get you started down that road, or help you get to the next rest stop.

For this lesson, you'll use the following items from the website that supports this book:

- Images: Photos in the Figure drawing and Heads folders; **Rhoda_brownstudy.jpg**

- Custom palette: **Gesture drawing.PAL** and **Rendering.PAL**

- Custom workspace: **Rhoda Gesture.pws**

Gesture Drawing

In a typical figure-drawing class, a nude model poses for increasing lengths of time, beginning with very short "gesture" poses lasting only a minute or two. Short poses can be very energetic and exciting to capture quickly with a few strokes. I often take my trusty MacBook Pro and a Wacom tablet to figure-drawing sessions. My hands stay clean and I don't have to worry about where to store all those drawings. Figure 8.1 shows some one-minute live gesture drawings I created in Painter. The model changes position so quickly that there's no time to think—or blink! There's certainly no time to make "corrections." But if you mess up, you've got a fresh start coming every 60 seconds.

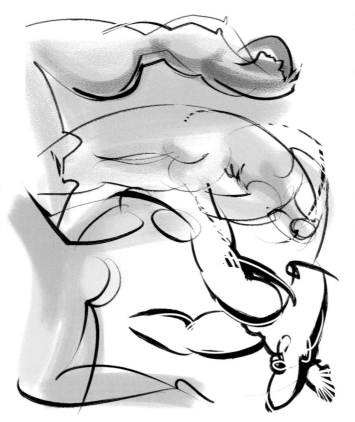

Figure 8.1
One-minute poses.

Quick and Clean

Short poses are meant to be warm-ups for the more important work of drawing anatomically accurate long poses. But for me, gestures are the main event. I attend a workshop where poses last a maximum of five minutes. In three hours I produce 40 or 50 drawings. They aren't all keepers, but many are worthy of printing or combining with others to create composite images. Several of them will inspire new work in oil or acrylic, the "messy" media.

A Quick Study

Keeping up the fast pace of gesture drawing requires a stripped-down workspace to maximize your efficiency and eliminate searching for tools, colors, and commands. I've created a custom workspace, called **Rhoda Gesture.pws**. Figure 8.2 shows what your desktop will look like after you import it. This workspace is designed for the 15-inch screen of my MacBook Pro. It includes a custom palette with my favorite brush variants, a paper texture, and the very important **Iterative Save** command. Feel free to make alterations to it, and save it with your own name. The image template I use, not part of the workspace, has a layer in **Gel** mode that is used for color, with dark strokes confined to the Corel Canvas.

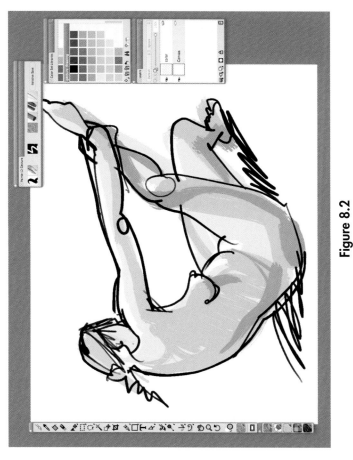

Figure 8.2
Gesture drawing workspace.

Take a closer look at the custom palette, shown in Figure 8.3. There are three variants for drawing lines on the canvas. **Dry Ink** and the **Scratchboard Tool** are both **Pen** variants, so I made custom icons for them to tell them apart at a glance. The sample strokes include some thin white lines drawn through a **Dry Ink** stroke. These were made with the **Scratchboard Tool** using white. I sometimes scratch away parts of my dark lines to add an energetic element. The two upper drawings in Figure 8.1 show that method.

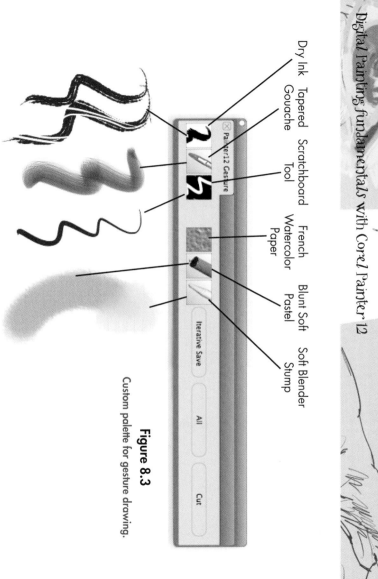

Dry Ink

Tapered
Gouache

Scratchboard
Tool

French
Watercolor
Paper

Blunt Soft
Pastel

Soft Blender
Stump

Figure 8.3
Custom palette for gesture drawing.

Make a **New Image** that fills most of your screen at 100% size, with enough room for the panels and palettes. Add a new **Layer** and choose **Gel** or **Multiply** method. Open **Rasa9.jpg**, shown in Figure 8.4. Using any of the variants on the left side of the custom palette, make a few quick strokes on the canvas to express the pose. Switch to the transparent layer and use either **Dry Ink** or **Pastel** to add color if it helps define the form. Save your sketch in **RIFF** format and clear the canvas (and layer) by pressing the **[Select] All** button followed by the **Cut** button. Now repeat the process, using a different combination of variants and colors. After each sketch, press the **Iterative Save** button and clear the canvas.

Your first few attempts might look like visual gibberish, but keep it up and you'll improve. Two of my efforts are shown in Figure 8.5. The image on the left was my fourth try, and the other was number seven.

Naked Truth

Being forced to work this quickly encourages you to focus on the essence of the pose, skipping details. Just as important, this kind of practice helps you plunge into the process and ignore any self-doubt about your skill. "Process, not product" is the mantra you need to repeat to yourself if you tend to judge your work negatively.

Figure 8.5
Don't erase, just try again.

Figure 8.4
A closed pose.

Ten Sketches in Ten Minutes

Open all ten of the images in the **Nudes** folder from the **Figure drawing** folder. Stack them in any order you like, just be sure they don't cover up the blank canvas you'll be working on. If you can get someone to time you and holler "next" every 60 seconds, you're good to go. Maybe there's a stopwatch app on your computer. Or set up a clock with a sweep second hand and keep one eye on it. Keep your other eye on the photo. Don't worry about not having a third eye to look at your drawing…peripheral vision should be enough.

For each photo, make only the essential strokes to capture the essence of the pose. If there is time, add color on the **Gel** layer, but only to enhance the energy of the gesture. Use the same method for saving and clearing the canvas that you just practiced. Close each photo as soon as you finish it with the shortcut **Cmd/Ctrl+W**.

Command Performance

To shave another second off your time for each drawing, you may want to add a **File > Close** command button to the custom palette. Just use the **Add Command** option in the **Custom Palette** menu. Be sure to choose the current palette as the destination for this new command.

All Hands on Deck

It could be a challenge to find people to get naked and pose for you while you practice your skills (check out figure-drawing workshops in your area). Easier to find, and something you always have with you, is your non-dominant hand. Pose it in various ways, with or without props. It should also be easy to get friends and family to give you a hand. Easiest of all, use the photos of my friends' hands and my hands, provided for you.

Start by sketching the hand in Figure 8.6. This time it's not about speed—take as much as five minutes! Add a **Pencil** variant, such as the **Real 6B Soft Pencil**, to your gesture palette. Sketch the hand in stages, similar to Figure 8.7, using shades of gray. Start with a rough placement of the main lines and shapes. Develop volume with crosshatching and shading. Use a **Gel** layer for the shading, if you wish. Make corrections as you go, using the **Scratchboard Tool** with white. Soften lines or hatching with the **Blender** stump. No tracing, no cloning!

Figure 8.6
Hand with curved fingers.

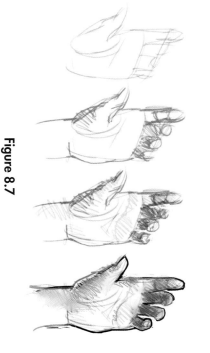

Figure 8.7
Sketching a hand.

Handy References

Practice drawing hands to learn proportion and hone your observation skills. The hand can be just as expressive and multi-faceted as the entire body.

Figure 8.8
Color film will be invented in about 80 years.

Animated Hands

Eadweard Muybridge, late-19th Century action photographer, left behind a treasure trove of photographs of people and animals doing everyday things like walking, running, and jumping. The series of Muybridge photos provided on the website that supports this book shows a hand picking up a ball. You'll use this sequence of 12 photos to practice quick gesture drawings of hands, and as a bonus you'll get some experience using some of Painter's Movie features.

The first photo in the sequence is shown in Figure 8.8. These photos are grainy and spotted, and were not meant to be artistic, but were used to examine motion scientifically. They are more than adequate to serve the purpose here, as clone sources.

Painter allows you to create a blank *framestack* from scratch by specifying the dimensions of the frames and the number of frames you want in the **Movie > New Movie** dialog box. Much better, for the purposes here, is opening the sequence of existing images as a framestack. The 12 Muybridge hand-and-ball frames have been numbered and are ready to load. Use **File > Open** and check the **Open Numbered Files** box. You'll be prompted to **Choose First Numbered File**, so you'll need to navigate to the folder that contains the sequence. When you choose **hand_01.jpg**, as shown in Figure 8.9, the prompt changes to request the **Last Numbered File**. Click **Open** and you'll get a **Save** dialog box, where you can give your movie a name and decide where to put it. The FRM format is assigned automatically.

Error Message?

Painter occasionally rejects your attempt to load perfectly numbered files as a framestack, by telling you the numbering is wrong. Take a deep breath and try again.

At this point your framestack will appear, along with its control panel, shown in Figure 8.10. Play the movie, which automatically loops over and over. Adjust the playback speed, designated in FPS (frames per second). About 10 FPS seems pleasing.

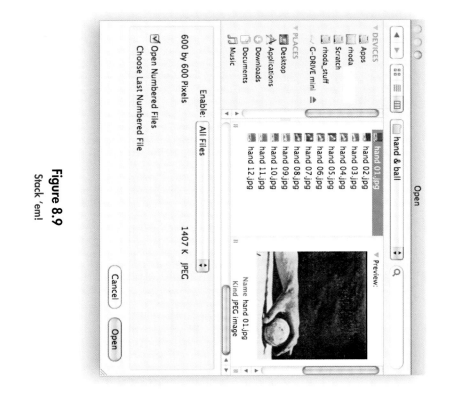

Figure 8.9
Stack 'em!

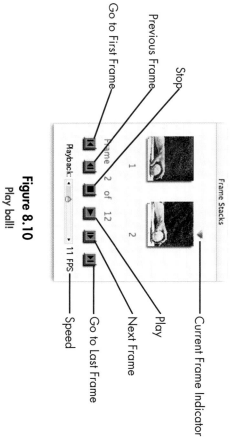

Figure 8.10
Play ball!

Previous Frame

Go to First Frame

Stop

Frame Stacks

Frame 2 of 12

1 2

Playback: 11 FPS

Current Frame Indicator

Play

Next Frame

Go to Last Frame

Speed

Just for fun, and as a quick and dirty way to get a peek at Painter's cel animation capabilities, put a smiley face on the ball. Better yet, have the smile change to a frown or a scream at the ball's highest point. Use bright red and a **Pen** variant. Figure 8.11 shows frame one, cropped, after this "enhancement." You probably accepted 2 as the default number of **Onion Skins** (a reference to traditional translucent paper), so when you have **Tracing Paper** on you can see both the current frame and one previous frame. This way, you can check the mouth expression in the previous frame, to make a smooth transition to the next. Use the **Next** and **Previous** frame buttons on the framestack controls. Figure 8.12 shows frame 10 is active with **Tracing Paper** on, so frame 9 is also visible. The smile is starting to fade.

Figure 8.11
Smiley.

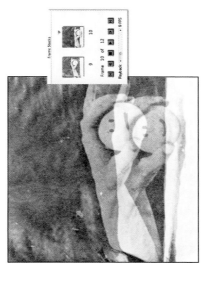

Figure 8.12
Not so smiley.

Rotoscoping

Traditional *rotoscoping* involves projecting a single frame from live action footage in perfect alignment with the animator's drawing surface. The animator draws each cel based on the action of the figure in the projected frame, and then steps forward to the next frame in the action to draw on the next cel. It's like sequential tracing with Painter's **Quick Clone** feature.

Make a new blank movie the same pixel dimensions and number of frames as the Muybridge framestack. Choose a color other than white in the **New Movie** dialog box, shown in Figure 8.13. (Resolution doesn't matter, because you won't be printing anything.) Make the Muybridge framestack the active movie and use the command **Set Movie Clone Source** in the **Movie** menu. Now return to the blank framestack and turn **Tracing Paper** on. You'll see a ghost image of the corresponding frame.

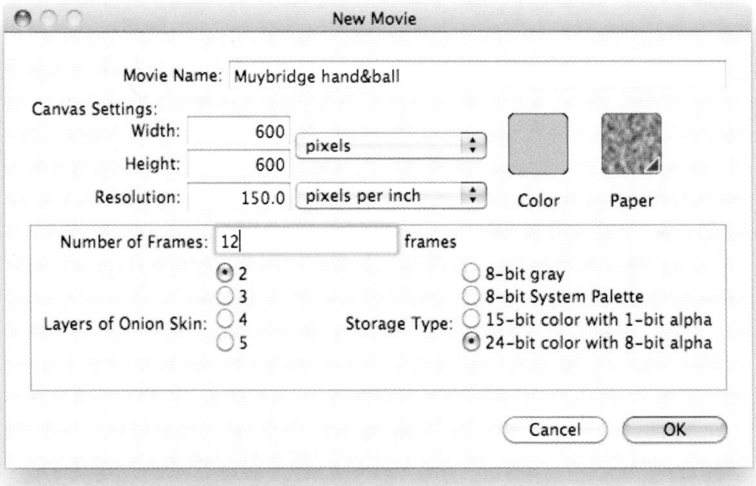

Use a **Pen** or **Pencil** variant to make energetic gesture drawings of the hand and ball in each frame. Start with frame 12, the last frame, and sketch each frame in a loose, scribbly style until you finish with frame one. Figure 8.14 shows my sketch of frame 12.

Figure 8.13
Make a new framestack.

Drawing Backwards

Why start drawing at the end of the stack? If you start on frame 1, you'll see the ghost of what you drew when you work on frame 2. That's great when you're animating from scratch, but you don't need the input from another frame when cloning or tracing. If you start at frame 12, there's nothing on frame 11 to get in the way.

Play your gesture movie. If you want to keep the ball rolling, repeat the process with a fresh framestack and use a different style, brush variant, or color. You can splice together several versions by using the **Insert Movie** command. The **Save As** option lets you convert your movie to a more versatile format, such as QuickTime or AVI, or save any frame as a still image.

Figure 8.14
Sketchy ball and hand.

New Movie

Movie Name: Muybridge hand&ball

Canvas Settings:
Width: 600 pixels
Height: 600 pixels
Resolution: 150.0 pixels per inch

Color   Paper

Number of Frames: 12 frames

Layers of Onion Skin:
○ 2
○ 3
○ 4
○ 5

Storage Type:
○ 8–bit gray
○ 8–bit System Palette
○ 15–bit color with 1–bit alpha
● 24–bit color with 8–bit alpha

Cancel   OK

Heads Up

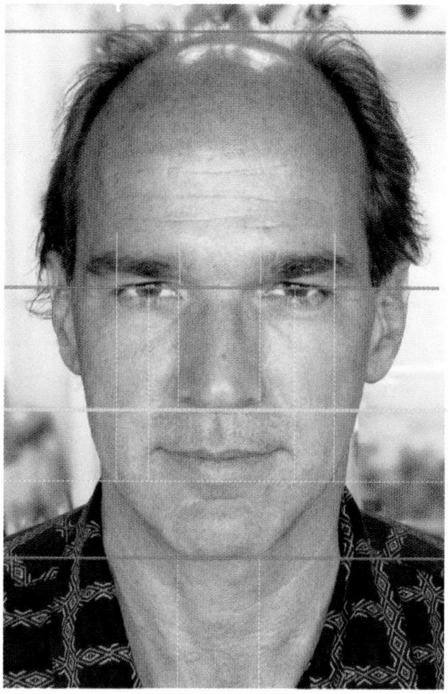

Drawing or painting a portrait without using tracing or cloning as "training wheels" will require not only careful observation but also a few guidelines about the proportions of the head and facial features. Notice the relative dimensions and relationships shown in Figure 8.15.

The horizontal lines in red show that the distance from the top of Barry's head to his eyes is the same as the distance from eyes to chin. The eyes-to-chin dimension is halved at the base of his nose, and the nose-to-chin length is equally divided at the bottom of the lip. For some vertical measurements, notice that the space between the eyes is about the same as the width of each eye. The tear ducts of the eyes line up with the wings of the nostrils. The centers of the pupils should line up with the corners of the mouth.

Of course there are individual variations due to ethnicity, gender, and age, but the divisions are remarkably consistent. At least they will help your portrait sketching get off on the right (um) foot. Barry's eyes appear to be somewhat widely spaced, compared to the statistical norms. Noticing such slight differences will help you capture a likeness, rather than a generic-looking face.

Figure 8.15
Face facts.

The Eyes Have It

Practice drawing individual features before you attempt to put them together. Let's start at the top and work down. Have someone take several photos of your face with a variety of emotional expressions, and then crop the photos to just the eyes. You can also practice using eyes in the **People > Heads > Eyes** folder. Do several studies of eye anatomy, starting with **Eyes_Barry.jpg**, shown in Figure 8.16.

Figure 8.16
Eyes front.

Eyes Right

The eyeball is a sphere, so its curvature must be described by darker shading near both corners. A deep shadow between the eye and bridge of the nose is created by the eye socket. The "shelf" of the lower eyelid tends to catch light, whereas the upper lid casts a shadow over the top of the eyeball. There is a slight bulge below the eye, to accommodate the lower part of the eyeball. In addition to a shiny spot on the pupil, there are also tiny highlights visible in the lachrymal gland, and the wet line where eyeball meets the lower eyelid. Find each of those elements in the drawings shown in Figure 8.17.

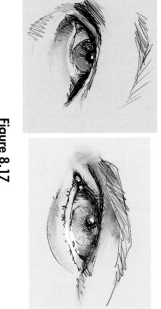

Figure 8.17
You lookin' at me?

Make a new image with a natural **Paper** texture and a tinted color, so you can create some lighter areas. You will make a detailed color sketch using the **Rendering.PAL** custom palette shown in Figure 8.18. These pencils are members of three different categories, all use **Cover** method, and work well together for drawings that suggest traditional pastels or charcoal.

Decide whether you want to draw the left or right eye. Make a rectangular selection of a portion of the eye photo (not to be confused with iPhoto) that has all the colors you'll need. Use **Make a New Color Set from Selection** in the **Color Set** menu. My color set for this project is shown in Figure 8.19.

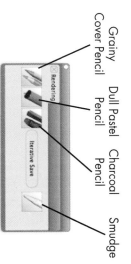

Grainy   Dull Pastel   Charcoal
Cover Pencil   Pencil   Pencil   Smudge

Figure 8.18
Three pencils and a smudge.

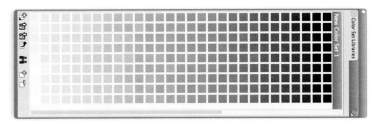

Figure 8.19
Color set in LHS.

Getting It Sorted

You'll find it much easier to choose the right color swatch with LHS sort order, available in the **Color Set** pop-up menu. This distributes the swatches primarily according to Lightness, rather than Hue or Saturation. Just go up higher on the set when you need a darker color, and lower down for a lighter one.

Choose the **Grainy Cover Pencil** and reduce its size to two or three pixels. Make some practice strokes with all three pencils and the **Smudge** tool, as shown in Figure 8.20.

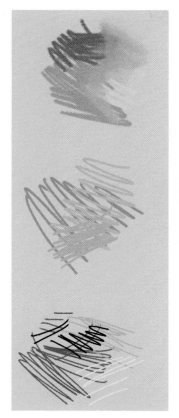

Figure 8.20
Batches of hatches.

Begin with a basic layout in a medium-dark color, smudging some areas to soften them. Switch to either the **Dull Pastel** or **Charcoal Pencil** variants to develop the forms. Apply hatches and crosshatches of color that follow the direction of the shapes. Blend some edges with the **Smudge** tool, but don't get too smooth. It's important for the viewer to see some of your pencil strokes. Return to the fine line **Grainy Cover Pencil** for eyelashes and eyebrow hairs.

Figure 8.21 shows the stages in rendering Barry's left eye.

Pick a Nose

Noses have a great deal of variation in structure, as shown in Figure 8.22. Once again, it pays to study classic nasal anatomy. You'll do a graphite pencil sketch of one of these items from **Noses.jpg**. But first, let's make a custom **Pencil** variant.

The swatch in Figure 8.23 shows the color used for making hatches and crosshatches with the **Sketching Pencil**. This variant uses **Buildup Method**, so strokes get dark very quickly. You will need to make more delicate lines, so reduce the default 5-pixel size to about 2 pixels. **Buildup Method** is fine, because the lines need to get darker as you develop forms, but change the **Subcategory** from **Grainy Hard Buildup** to **Soft Buildup**. This will ensure smooth strokes regardless of paper texture. Figure 8.24 shows the change in the **General Brush Controls** panel.

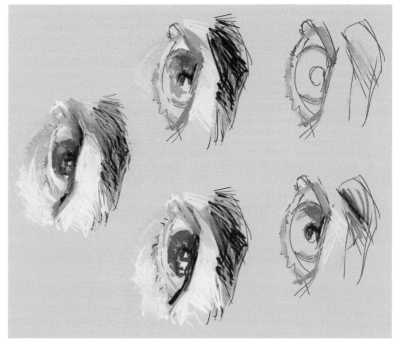

Figure 8.21
Eye chart.

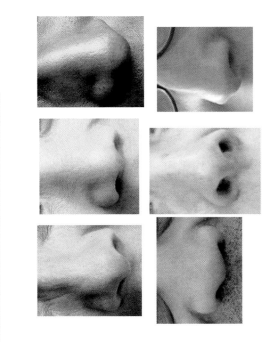

Figure 8.23
Buildup hatches.

Figure 8.22
Contemplate your nasal.

Figure 8.24
Soft buildup.

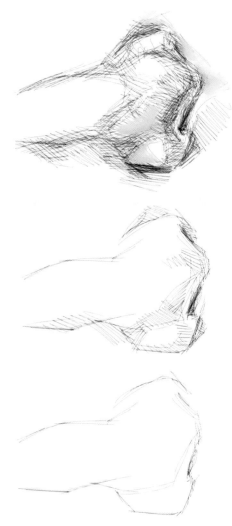

Figure 8.25
Nasal passages.

Save your new pencil as **Graphite** or **Rendering Pencil**, using the **Save Variant** command in the **Brushes** menu. You may want to add it to your Rendering custom palette. Open the **Noses.jpg** photo and use your new pencil to sketch the example in the upper left. Remember to choose a gray color to enhance the effect of a graphite drawing. Figure 8.25 shows stages in developing the sketch from a simple blocking in of basic structure to more depth and tonality.

156

Lip Service

The mouth is even more expressive than the eyes, and there are variations in structure as well as in the relative sizes of lips and their curvature. Figure 8.26 shows a few samples. Draw several of them in either graphite or colored pencil style. My sketch of Martin's mouth (in the upper right) is a combination of the custom **Graphite** pencil plus **Grainy Cover** pencil for the light blue touches to indicate highlights and some of the whiskery bits. Figure 8.27 shows this working nicely on blue paper.

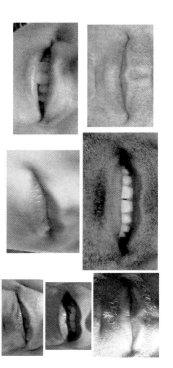

Figure 8.26
Oral majority.

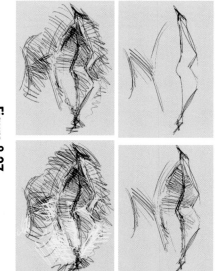

Figure 8.27
Martin's mouth.

Altogether Now

Using your newly acquired or sharpened skills, draw either a graphite sketch or color rendering of the photo, **Rhoda_brownstudy.jpg**, shown in Figure 8.28. One challenge is working with features that are at an angle, another is getting all the individual parts in the right place. Use a preliminary sketch layer if you want to block in the basic elements. In keeping with my tradition of including at least one self-portrait in every edition of this book, I invite you to practice on my face and then do one of yourself.

Make a new image the same dimensions as the photo. Dull green will make a good paper color, so choose one and use the **Set Paper Color** command in the **Canvas** menu. **Select All** (**Cmd/Ctrl+A**) and **Delete/Backspace** to fill the blank image with the new paper color.

My first attempt isn't quite right, and reveals that 40 years as a professional caricature artist has given me some habits of exaggeration. To help make corrections, enable the **Layout Grid** from the **Composition** panels. With the photo and preliminary sketch side by side, it's much easier to see what needs adjusting. Figure 8.29 shows the areas that need the most fixing. If you need to make a lot of repairs, create another layer and turn the opacity of the first sketch way down.

Figure 8.28
Rhoda Draws!

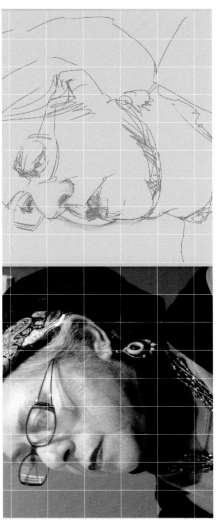

Figure 8.29
Grid your lines.

Compare both sketches to see how much change was needed. This might help you learn to estimate placement, sizes, and angles better next time. Figure 8.30 shows corrections made with the help of a grid.

This will be a pastel sketch, similar in style to the eye study you did earlier. Add a few variants to the rendering custom palette, as shown in Figure 8.31. You'll need a larger size **Pastel** and/or **Conte**, and a more robust **Blender**. To tell them apart from the other variants with identical icons, right-click (**Ctrl**-click) and choose **View as Text**. Sample strokes were made on the gray-green paper.

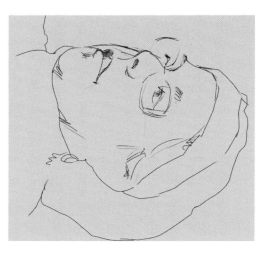

Figure 8.30
Rhoda Drawn better!

Figure 8.31
Portrait palette.

Make a new layer for color, and move the sketch layer above it, so it can serve as a guide for the next stage. Apply patches of color with the **Square Grainy Pastel** and **Dull Conte**, blending them a little as you go. Figure 8.32 shows the first color patches and Figure 8.33 shows the **Layers** palette at this point.

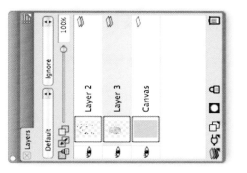

Figure 8.32
Show us your patches.

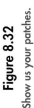

Figure 8.33
Sketch layer on top.

Figure 8.34
A patchwork face.

When you have most of the color patches established, as shown in Figure 8.34, use the **Mixer** to create intermediate colors. To change the color of a swatch in the **Mixer**, use the **Dropper** from the **Toolbox** (not from the **Mixer**) to sample a color from your painting, then press the **Cmd/Ctrl** key as you click on a swatch in the **Mixer**. When all the swatches you want are changed, use **Apply Color** and **Mix Color** to make all the color combinations needed, as shown in Figure 8.35.

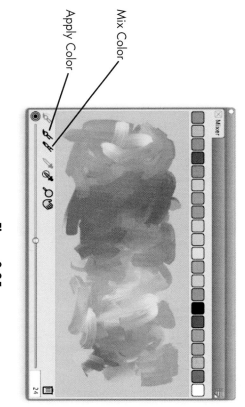

Mix Color

Apply Color

Figure 8.35
Mix it up.

Color Scheming

Using commands in the **Mixer** pop-up menu, you can change the background color of the **Mixer Pad** to match your paper. You can save **Mixer** colors and also create a **Color Set** from your **Mixer Pad**.

The stage shown in Figure 8.36 has most of the skin tones blended and the beginning of details made with the **Charcoal Pencil** and **Dull Pastel Pencil**. The finished portrait, shown in Figure 8.37, has refined many areas and added tiny details with the **Grainy Cover Pencil**. The eyes are a challenge, because they are half closed and partially hidden by the glasses. I used some dark blue to hint at the color of my eyes and a few thin lines for lashes that are of a lighter color. Notice the loose indications for the jewelry and the brocade pattern of the hat. Some of the outer edges are just as rough as they were in the earliest stage. This is not a sign that I got bored, but a traditional technique for making the focal point sections that are more developed.

Figure 8.36
Likeness emerging.

Figure 8.37
Rhoda Drawn!

What's Next?

In the next set of assignments, in Lesson 9, "Fine Art Explorations," you'll continue exploring fine art techniques. Abstract painting will give you a break from reality, and you'll take the plunge into Painter 12's new Watercolor brushes.

Fine Art Explorations

The challenge in traditional drawing and painting is making your work look like the subject, with a great deal of wiggle room for interpretation and style. The challenge in abstract art is making your work *not* look like the subject, or (depending on your definition of abstract), not even having a subject. You'll have the opportunity to do both of these in this set of lessons.

For this lesson, you'll use the following items from the website that supports this book:

- Images: **Heliconia.jpg, Glassware.jpg,** and **BubbleWrap.jpg**

- Custom palettes: **DigitalWatercolor.PAL, RealWatercolor.PAL, Abstract_Photo.PAL,** and **MixedMedia.PAL**

Water World

Painter 12 offers three brush categories for emulating watercolor effects. You'll explore two of them by creating the same painting twice. Painter's legacy watercolor brushes are called **Digital Watercolor**. There are 29 variants for this category, way more than you're ever likely to need. Figure 9.1 shows strokes produced by 11 of them with the same blue color. The **Digital Watercolor** custom palette provided for you has six of those, with custom icons made from the practice strokes. Use the **Custom Palette Organizer** to import it, or make your own from the variants shown in Figure 9.2. Spend a few minutes playing with these variants, and any or all of the remaining 23 in the **Digital Watercolor** group.

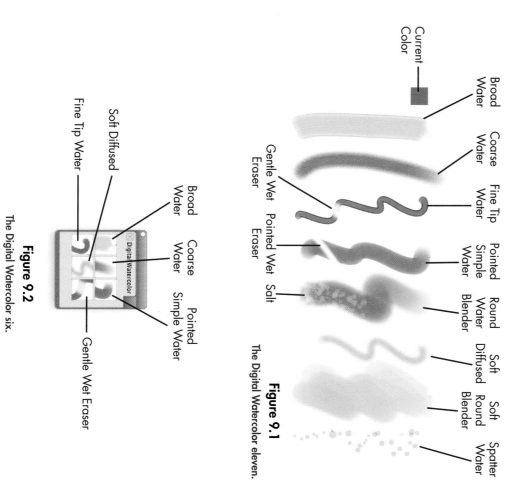

Current
Color

Broad
Water

Coarse
Water

Fine Tip
Water

Pointed
Simple
Water

Round
Water
Blender

Soft
Diffused
Round
Blender

Spatter
Water

Gentle Wet
Eraser

Pointed Wet
Eraser

Salt

Figure 9.1
The Digital Watercolor eleven.

Fine Tip Water

Soft Diffused

Broad
Water

Coarse
Water

Pointed
Simple Water

Gentle Wet Eraser

Figure 9.2
The Digital Watercolor six.

The qualities that help make **Digital Watercolor** variants convincing include transparency, diffusion of paint into the paper grain, and the "wet fringe" effect—pooling of pigment along the edges of a brushstroke. Figure 9.3 shows a close-up of strokes that demonstrate the diffusion and wet fringe phenomena.

Figure 9.3
Diffusion and fringe.

Wade in the Water

Let's create a watercolor painting of the beautiful Hawaiian Heliconia plant, shown in Figure 9.4. Open **Heliconia.jpg** and resize it if needed. Use **File > Quick Clone** to have access to tracing paper. Adjust **Tracing Paper Opacity** as desired with the slider on the **Clone Source** panel. Make a new layer and draw a simple sketch of the photo with dark green and a **Pencil** variant, similar to the one shown in Figure 9.5. This sketch layer will serve to provide guidelines for your painting as you look at the photo for color reference. Do not use **Clone Color** (trust me, it's for your own good)! You do have my permission to create a new **Color Set** from the photo or a small selection that includes all the basic greens, reds, and yellows.

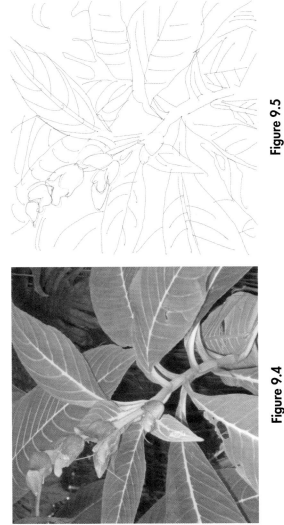

Figure 9.5
Sketch layer.

Figure 9.4
Heliconia plant.

Imitation of Light

Techniques that enable you to emulate the luminosity of watercolor painting include building up color from light to dark, applying thin layers of pigment, and allowing bits of white paper to remain untouched. Choice of **Paper** texture will also enhance the effect. Try each of the four **Watercolor Papers** that load with the default library.

Make a new layer. **Digital Watercolor** works on standard layers, not the special **Watercolor Layer** used by the other two categories. Use the **Broad Water** variant to apply the first coat of paint, with pale greens, yellows, pinks, and light brown for the background leaves. **Digital Watercolor** strokes automatically switch the layer **Composite Method** to **Gel**. This is essential to creating the look of transparency. Figure 9.6 shows this early stage, and Figure 9.7 shows the current **Layers** panel.

Figure 9.6
Transparent paint.

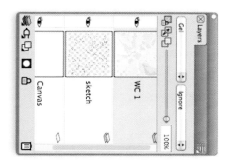

Figure 9.7
There's always room for Gel mode.

Use several shades of green for visual variety as you build up color. Figure 9.8 shows the painting with several leaves developed to the next stage. Notice that the second layer of strokes deliberately avoids coloring the veins of the leaves, which are meant to remain very light. A medium olive green has been added to establish the areas that will become the darkest tones.

Figure 9.8
Build from light to dark.

Accentuate the Negative

Those dark areas where the deep shadows appear are important elements of the composition. Artists call them *negative shapes*, but they make a positive contribution to your painting.

Make another new layer, WC2, for additional watercolor painting. This will have the effect of "drying" the WC1 layer. Continue to develop color and add some detail with smaller variants. Figure 9.9 shows a stage with richer color for the flowers on the WC1 layer and much darker background areas on the new layer. The background sections have actually become a bit too dark. Staying within the watercolor paradigm, treat it like wet paint and try to mop some of it up. Using **Broad Water** and a light color, you can soak up some of the pigment. Figure 9.10 shows the center section of layer WC2 before and after the repair.

Figure 9.9
Too dark, perhaps.

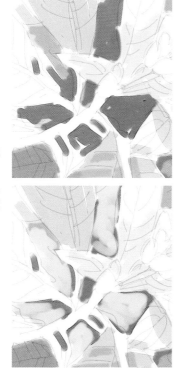

Figure 9.10
Paint remover.

Take Back the Light

Traditional watercolorists have a number of tricks for removing pigment. If the paint is still wet, a sponge or paper towel can suck up the excess. Even after the paint is dry, scrubbing with a wet sponge can work. Careful scraping with a sharper tool can reveal areas of white paper once again. Painter provides options in the **Layers** menu to dry the entire **Digital Watercolor** layer.

The finished painting, with the sketch layer deleted, is shown in Figure 9.11. You may want to keep the sketch layer, at a lower opacity, as part of your finished work.

Figure 9.11
Heliconia completed.

Deep Water

Now that you've splashed around in the kiddy pool, you're ready to really dive in. Switch to the brand new, most sophisticated watercolor category, **Real Watercolor**. Figure 9.12 shows several of the variants, but what it can't show is how some of these brushes behave on their way to their final color. **Real Wet Wash**, for example, starts out with the current color, then shrinks and lightens up as if it is being absorbed into the paper. **A Fractal Wash Wet** stroke also lightens up and changes a few seconds after it is applied. This variant creates some amazingly realistic effects, including the mottling and "blooms" that can occur when paper has different degrees of wetness. **Rough Edges** manages to remove color in the center and create very irregular fringes. Play with the amazing **Real Watercolor** variants for a while.

Figure 9.13 shows the custom palette for **Real Watercolor**. Those eight variants will give you plenty of opportunity to experiment as you create another version of **Heliconia**. Use the same preliminary sketch as before.

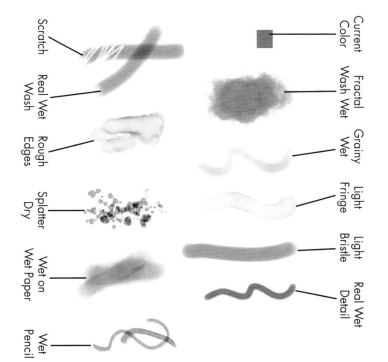

Current Color

Fractal Wash Wet

Grainy Wet

Light Fringe

Light Bristle

Real Wet Detail

Scratch

Real Wet Wash

Rough Edges

Splatter Dry

Wet on Wet Paper

Wet Pencil

Figure 9.12
Eleven Real Watercolor brushes.

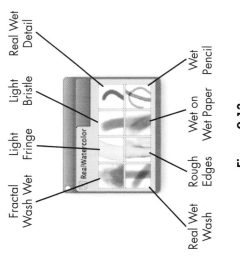

Fractal Wash Wet — Light Fringe — Light Bristle — Real Wet Detail

Real Wet Wash — Rough Edges — Wet on Wet Paper — Wet Pencil

Figure 9.13
Then there were eight.

A Special Layer

When you apply a **Real Watercolor** stroke, Painter automatically creates a layer reserved only for these special variants. Not surprisingly, it is in **Gel** mode, for transparency. If you try to paint on a **Watercolor** layer with brushes from other categories, you'll get a warning (but not a ticket).

Your approach should be similar to how you handled the **Digital Watercolor** painting, but there are bound to be differences in the result due to the widely different behaviors of the brushes in each category. For the first stage, shown in Figure 9.14, lay down large rough areas of color with **Fractal Wash Wet.** I also painted a stem with the **Light Bristle** variant.

Figure 9.14
Your wash is wet.

Build up color and develop the forms by adding strokes with **Wet on Wet Paper** and **Real Wet Wash**. Use **Light Bristle** to add richer color to leaves, allowing the veins to remain untouched. If some areas get too dark, choose a light color and mop up with some **Rough Edges** strokes. Figure 9.15 shows the work in progress.

Add a **New Watercolor** layer for the next stage. Turn off the visibility of the sketch, too. The darkest background areas can be completed with **Real Wet Wash**. Use **Real Wet Detail** and **Wet Pencil** for bold lines and crisp edges, and also to provide some veins for the leaves. Figure 9.16 shows only the second **Watercolor** layer, with visibility of the first one turned off. The finished piece is shown in Figure 9.17.

Figure 9.15
Still rough around the edges.

Figure 9.16
Layer two.

Figure 9.17
Heliconia revisited.

Less Is More

The design principle that simplicity can be more effective than ornamentation applies in painting, too. You don't need to include every vein on every leaf. Leave something to the imagination of the viewer.

Abstract Painting

There is a difference between abstract and non-objective art. To oversimplify, "abstract" is reserved for artwork that is based in reality, whereas "non-objective" is, well, not based on anything. It's just a collection of lines, shapes, tones, and textures. The essential elements for creating any kind of art are the same:

- **Line:** So many possibilities—straight or curved, smooth or jagged, bold or timid (I could go on)

- **Shape:** Large or small, geometric or organic, simple or complex....

- **Tone (Color):** Dark or light, saturated or dull, warm or cool....

- **Texture:** Rough or smooth, subtle or strong, natural or synthetic....

Categories can overlap: a line that curves back on itself or is very fat becomes a shape. Lots of lines close together make a texture, and so on. The artist's job is to work out how to organize those elements on the canvas. A few basic principles, in no particular order, will help with that:

- **Contrast:** Not just brightness differences, but contrast in size, texture, or complexity of elements to create visual variety.

- **Repitition:** Create unity by repeating some of the elements, with variation in size, color, and angle.

- **Balance:** Composition, or placement of elements so that they work well within the picture plane.

- **Focal Point:** Create at least one center of interest, so it's not just wallpaper.

Grounded in Reality

Let's begin with an existing image—just about any subject will do. There are several photos in the **Things** folder on the website that are nearly abstract already. Find them in a folder called **Abstract This!**

Your goal is to create a painting that begins with a photo or image composite, borrows freely from its visual elements, and goes off in its own direction. Start with **Glassware.jpg**, shown in Figure 9.18. Resize it to fit on your screen at 100% magnification. I reduced the size to about 1100 pixels wide. This photo of glass pitchers has an interesting combination of shapes and an excellent range of tonality from bright white to solid black.

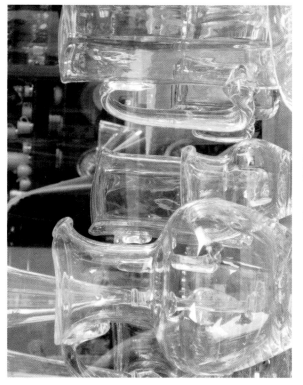

Figure 9.18
Grounded glass.

That big black area is a bit too strong, actually. Soften it by pasting the **BubbleWrap.jpg** photo over it as a layer. The photo of a huge roll of bubblewrap works as a textured gradient from light to dark. Choose **Lighten** as the composite method and reduce the opacity of the layer to about 70%. This reduces contrast for the time being, but you will create dark areas where you want them later. Figure 9.19 shows the composite, and Figure 9.20 shows the **Layers** palette at this stage.

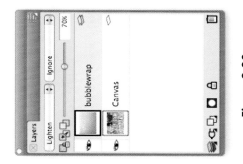

Figure 9.20
Lighten up.

Figure 9.19
Wrapped glass.

Blending the Truth

The custom palette for this project, **Abstract_Photo**, is shown in Figure 9.21. It has a couple of brush variants for smearing, another for darkening colors, and a **Cloner** for retrieving pixels from an earlier state. Use **File > Clone** to make a copy of the composite. You'll work on the copy and use the original as a safety net. Choose the **Smeary Varnish** brush and go nuts! Smear away, but try to follow the contours of the glass shapes. Figure 9.22 shows the smeared image. Because **Smeary Varnish** is an **Impasto** brush, there is depth and thickness to the bristly strokes. These will look best at 100% magnification.

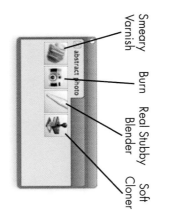

Smeary   Burn   Real Stubby   Soft
Varnish   Blender   Cloner

Figure 9.21
Smears, Burns, and Cloner, a law firm.

Figure 9.22
Impasto galore!

Pass the Impasto

Impasto is an Italian term both for the process of applying paint thickly, and for the result—strokes that have depth. You can hide or show **Impasto** depth with a setting in the **Navigator** panel. Earlier versions have a depth toggle readily available on the upper right edge of the image window. For more **Impasto** controls, use **Canvas > Surface Lighting**, shown in Figure 9.23.

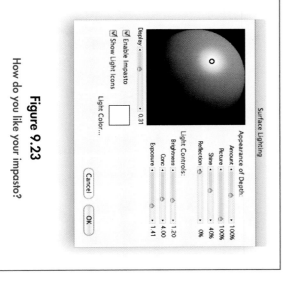

Figure 9.23
How do you like your impasto?

Save this version and make a clone copy once again. The photos had only very subtle color to begin with. A global increase in color on the entire image is worth a try. Open **Auto-Painting panels > Underpainting**, shown in Figure 9.24, and move the **Saturation** slider up to 75%. So much color just waiting to be revealed! The effect is shown in Figure 9.25. It's easy to desaturate some areas if you wish, by simply using the **Soft Cloner** to paint pixels from the previous version back in.

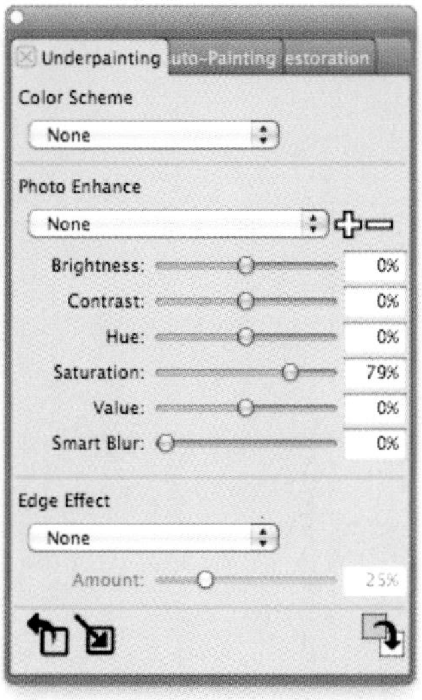

Figure 9.24
Increase saturation.

Figure 9.25
Brilliant colors emerge.

Compare and Contrast

More tonal contrast is called for at this point, and the **Burn** variant of the **Photo** brush category will do the trick. Figure 9.26 shows darker areas created with the **Burn** brush.

Figure 9.26
Tonal contrast restored.

177

Another kind of contrast involves texture. The painting is almost completely covered with striated impasto strokes. Perhaps some smooth, flat areas would help create some rest areas for the eye. Use the **Real Stubby Blender** in the custom palette to smooth out some spots. Recall that size can be useful for enhancing contrast, so create some variety in the size (and direction) of your blending strokes. Once again, use **File > Clone** to work on a copy, while the current version serves as backup. Figure 9.27 has some smooth areas. Be careful not to blend away the interesting details inside the oval at the lower left. These can serve as a major focal point.

Notice the bits of turquoise near the left edge. This color hardly appears elsewhere in the painting. Here's an opportunity to create some repetition. Choose the **Burn** tool in the custom palette, but don't use it. Instead, switch to the **Colorizer** variant in the same category (**Photo**). Sample the turquoise with the **Dropper** tool and use the **Colorizer** in several areas. This brush will not change the tonality (brightness) of pixels, just their hue. Figure 9.28 shows a detail of the painting with turquoise strokes added. Use this technique if you want to alter colors anywhere else in the image.

Figure 9.27
Smooth moves.

Figure 9.28
Colorize me!

This almost looks good enough to print. Let's add a white border, using the **Canvas > Canvas Size** command. About 50 pixels added to each side works. The straight, clean edges of the image look too mechanical. Fix that with the **Smeary Varnish** brush. The final version appears in Figure 9.29.

Consider printing your finished painting on canvas, then adding traditional oil or acrylic paint strokes for a truly mixed media piece. See Appendix A for other printing options and resources.

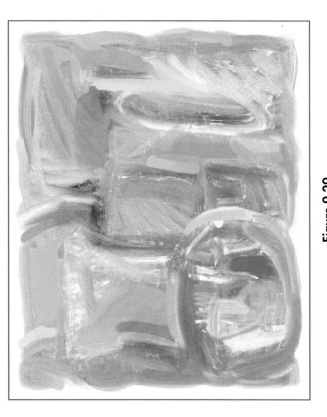

Figure 9.29
Don't neglect your edges.

Drawing a Blank

For a non-objective painting, you'll begin with a blank canvas (and an equally blank mind, if possible). Create a new canvas at a convenient size to fit your screen. Make it square, so you can avoid even the suggestion of "portrait" or "landscape" as subject matter. Many painters like to begin with a toned canvas or tinted paper, which are not quite as intimidating as pure white.

Limit your brush choices to a manageable number by using the **Mixed Media** custom palette shown in Figure 9.30. Each of the seven brushes is from a different category, so there's no need to create custom icons to tell them apart. Also included is a Paper texture, **Small Dots**.

■ Real Bristle Brushes > Real Fan Soft

■ Artists Oils > Clumpy Brush

■ Acrylics > Real Wet Brush

■ Blenders > Soft Blender Stump 30

■ Impasto > Smeary Flat

■ Pastels > Square Hard Pastel 40

■ Conte > Real Hard Conte

Strokes from each of these brushes are shown in Figure 9.31 on the tan paper I chose. Take some time to get familiar with each of these variants by scribbling with them on your tinted canvas. Explore how they interact with each other. Use different textures for the **Pastel** and **Conte** sticks.

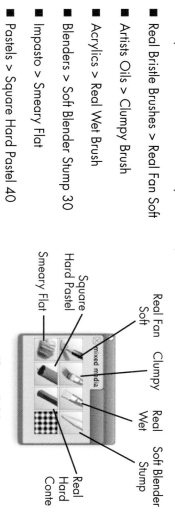

Figure 9.30
The Mixed Media custom palette.

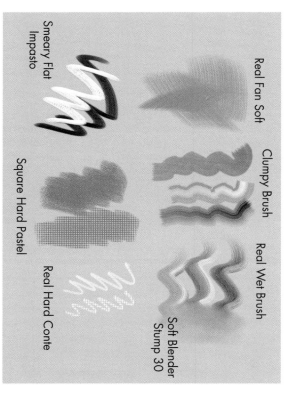

Figure 9.31
Practice strokes.

If you're wondering how to achieve multi-colored strokes for the **Clumpy** and **Real Wet** brushes, you'll need to open the **Mixer**, one of the **Color** panels. Figure 9.32 shows the **Mixer** with customized color swatches. I'll be working with a limited palette of red-oranges and browns. Basic black and white are included, too. Change the default swatches in the **Mixer** by choosing or sampling a color you like and pressing **Cmd/Ctrl** as you click on the swatch you want to replace.

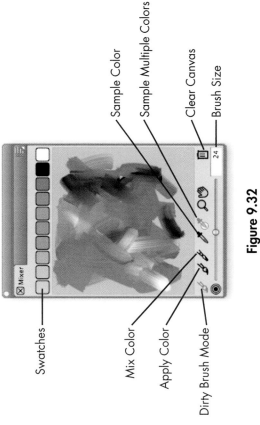

Swatches

Sample Color

Sample Multiple Colors

Clear Canvas

Brush Size

Mix Color

Apply Color

Dirty Brush Mode

Figure 9.32
Show us your swatches.

The **Mixer Pad** is the area under the swatches where you can apply colors and mix them (with a palette knife!) to generate new colors that can be sampled for painting. The **Sample Multiple Colors** tool is the crucial one for creating multi-colored strokes with certain brush variants. Use it to click an area on the **Mixer Pad** where two or more colors meet. Enlarge **Brush Size** if needed.

By now, you probably have quite a bit of test scribbling on your canvas. Okay, this will be the beginning of your non-objective painting! Mine is shown in Figure 9.33. Yours will be very different, of course, but we will both have the same challenges. We will be using shape, line, tone, and texture to produce a coherent work with visual contrast as well as balance and a focal point or two. What could possibly go wrong?

First take a good long look at your scribbles and decide what you like and what you'd like to eliminate. Some of mine will have to be smeared away or painted over. And I will extend much closer to the edges of the canvas. Use **Iterative Save (Cmd/Ctrl+Opt/Alt+S)** to keep each stage in your process as the work develops.

The next stage, shown in Figure 9.34, has established three quiet corners of mostly smooth color with the **Square Pastel** and the **Basic Paper** texture. The upper one third is under better control.

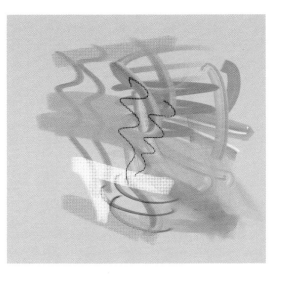

Figure 9.34
Get it under control.

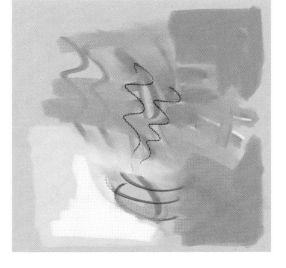

Figure 9.33
My two-year old could do that!

Painting solid color on the lower left has emphasized the impasto depth of the **Smeary Flat** brush strokes. (It isn't the strokes of this **Impasto** variant that are flat, but the shape of the brush tip.) They echo the black scribbles of the **Conte** stick. Repetition is one way to create visual interest.

Noticing that my strokes tend to appear in groups of two, I will make that another kind of repetition. Figure 9.35 shows the next stage with two strong vertical strokes at the top and a couple of squares drawn with the **Conte** stick at the bottom. The bold texture was made by increasing the scale of the **Small Dots** to very large dots, using the **Papers** panel.

As the work progresses, consider what might be needed next. More texture or contrast? Does something need to be bigger or smaller? Darker or lighter? At some point you'll have to decide when you're finished. That can be the biggest challenge of all. Figure 9.36 shows my end result.

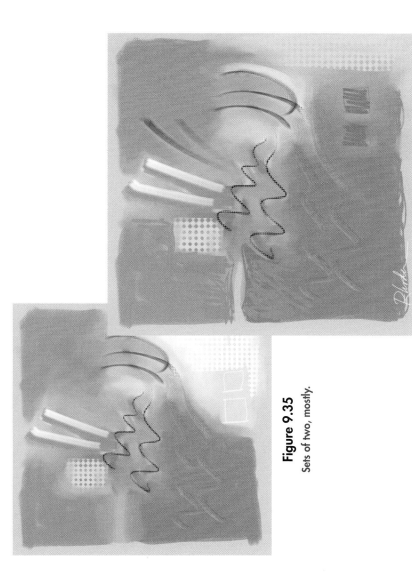

Figure 9.35
Sets of two, mostly.

Figure 9.36
It's done when you sign it.

What's Next?

Congratulations on making it through an intense lesson requiring you to stretch your skills and imagination. I invite you to come back and repeat some of these projects again with different source images or brush categories. Take your best paintings from this session and print them on canvas or watercolor paper specially made for desktop inkjet printers. If you want to produce large output, see the resource section in Appendix A.

In the next lesson, you'll continue to experiment with other exciting Painter features, and you'll meet the guest artist.

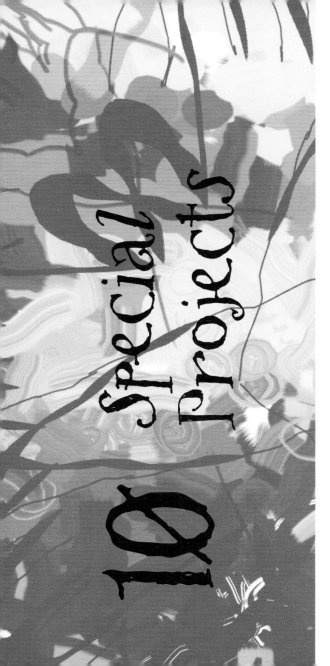

10 Special Projects

Would you like to give Painter a bit more control over your artwork? You'll want to play around with **Auto-Painting** and **Smart Strokes.** If you're interested in more efficient use of your time, let Painter give you a two-fer—make two strokes for the price of one with version 12's new **Mirror Painting** features. But first, let's look over the very talented shoulder of Stewart McKissick, to see how he creates a humorous illustration from start to finish. Remember the imaginary landscape you made in Lesson 4, "The Great 'scape"? Stewart takes Painter's **Airbrush** capability to a whole 'nuther level!

For this lesson, you'll use the following items from the website that supports this book:

- Images: **Martin.jpg** and **Radial_hands.jpg**

Presidents' Day Cartoon (by Stewart McKissick)

Trained as a traditional illustrator, I began using digital media, especially Painter, to finish my illustrations in the mid 1990s. I love the large variety of brushes that imitate existing art materials, combined with all the wonderful advantages digital media gives an artist to experiment freely. My long-time favorite saying about digital art is "It's not what it *does*, it's what it *UN-does!*"

I've worked in many styles over the years, but humorous work has always been my favorite. The idea for this piece that I call "Presidents' Day" came to me partly from the illustrations of J. C. Leyendecker, who painted many covers for *The Saturday Evening Post* in the early 20th century featuring comical babies for New Year's and Thanksgiving holiday issues. The finished art is shown in Figure 10.1.

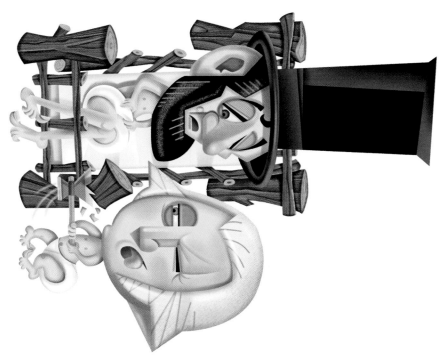

Figure 10.1
Looking presidential.

Figure 10.2
Analog drawing.

Pencil Drawing

I always start with a pencil drawing, shown in Figure 10.2. I make many thumbnail sketches and do research to help me resolve the idea and refine the composition—in this case, lots of pictures of Washington and Lincoln. Washington's face I based on the famous Gilbert Stuart portrait. I aggressively stylize shapes for (hopefully) comic effect. I re-traced my drawing several times to refine it. My drawings are pretty small so they can fit on a flatbed scanner.

I scan the finished drawing and open it in Painter. I always use RIFF format so all of Painters' layers and special features will be preserved during the working process.

I **Select >All** and **Select > Float** to put the drawing on its own Layer. I choose **Gel** from the **Composite Method** list. Now it's transparent and I can see through it to the canvas and other layers that I'll make later. I can also turn its visibility on and off as I wish using the eye icon on the layer.

Creating Shapes

My favorite method of working in a cartoon style in Painter involves using the **Pen** tool to create **Shapes**. Figure 10.3 shows the **Pen** tool selected. The **Pen** tool works by placing **Anchor Points** and **Wings** to draw line and curve segments. Figure 10.4 shows that a shape for Washington's head can be made with four anchor points. It takes some practice to learn this tool, as it has no "traditional" media equivalent. Once you master it, you can draw very precise shapes quickly and edit them as much as you want, by dragging the wings around with those little handles at the ends. The **Shape Selector** tool (the white arrow) lets you move and modify the points and wings.

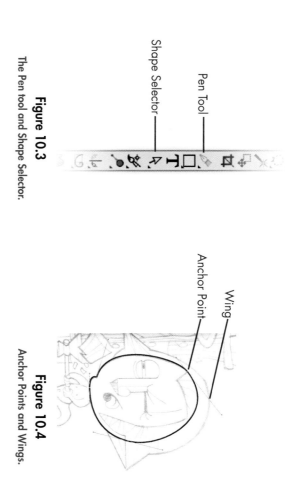

Figure 10.3

The Pen tool and Shape Selector.

Pen Tool

Shape Selector

Figure 10.4

Anchor Points and Wings.

Wing

Anchor Point

Airbrush Technique

Using this approach I am basically working the way a traditional artist would, using an airbrush and "friskets," or masks, to protect some areas of the canvas while painting in others. This can result in very clean hard edges where you want them.

Shapes made with the **Pen** tool are each on their own special layer, as shown in Figure 10.5. You can retain them as **Shapes** with **Strokes** and flat-color **Fills** or turn them into **Selections** using the button on the **Property Bar**, shown in Figure 10.6, which appears when you have the **Pen** tool or **Shape Selector** tool chosen. You'll see the outline of the shape turn into the moving dashed line or "marching ants," as in Figure 10.7.

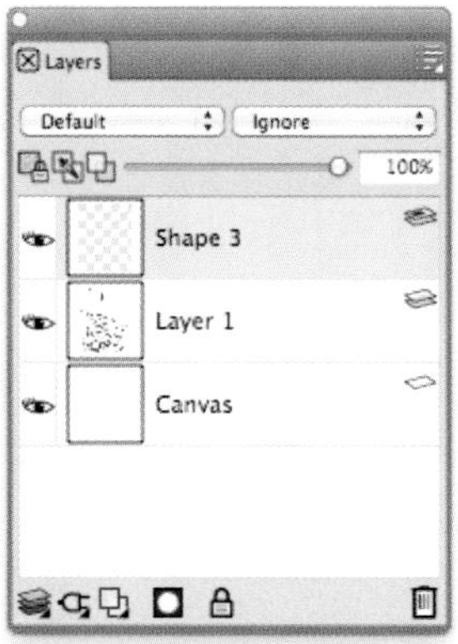

Figure 10.5

Shapes have a special layer.

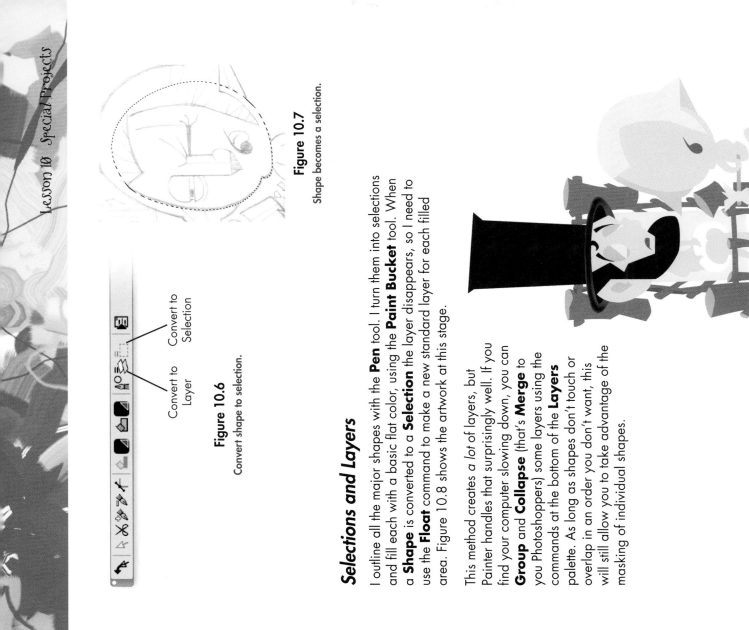

Convert to Layer

Convert to Selection

Figure 10.6
Convert shape to selection.

Figure 10.7
Shape becomes a selection.

Figure 10.8
Solid color fills.

Selections and Layers

I outline all the major shapes with the **Pen** tool. I turn them into selections and fill each with a basic flat color, using the **Paint Bucket** tool. When a **Shape** is converted to a **Selection** the layer disappears, so I need to use the **Float** command to make a new standard layer for each filled area. Figure 10.8 shows the artwork at this stage.

This method creates *a lot* of layers, but Painter handles that surprisingly well. If you find your computer slowing down, you can **Group** and **Collapse** (that's **Merge** to you Photoshoppers) some layers using the commands at the bottom of the **Layers** palette. As long as shapes don't touch or overlap in an order you don't want, this will still allow you to take advantage of the masking of individual shapes.

Shading

At this point I begin to shade the individual shapes, using the **Digital Airbrush**. This soft-edged brush most closely resembles a traditional airbrush. To keep the shading only on the shape on the chosen layer, you can re-select it by going to the **Select** menu and choosing **Load Selection**. Then choose **Layer Transparency** in the **Load From** box and **Replace Selection** from the **Operation** list, as shown in Figure 10.9. A shortcut is to Control+click (right-click in Windows) on the desired layer's name in the **Layers** palette. This automatically loads the layer's contents as a selection.

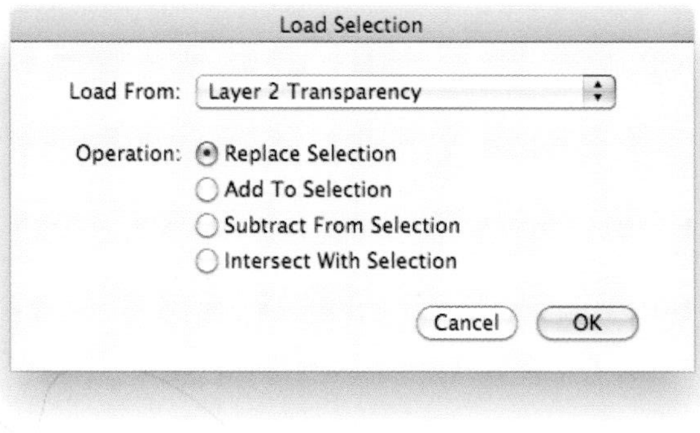

Figure 10.9
Load selection.

No Painting Allowed on Transparent Pixels

Alternately, you can paint new strokes only on the colored areas by choosing the **Preserve Transparency** button on the **Layers** palette, shown in Figure 10.10. But don't forget to uncheck the button if you make a new blank layer, or you won't be able to paint on it!

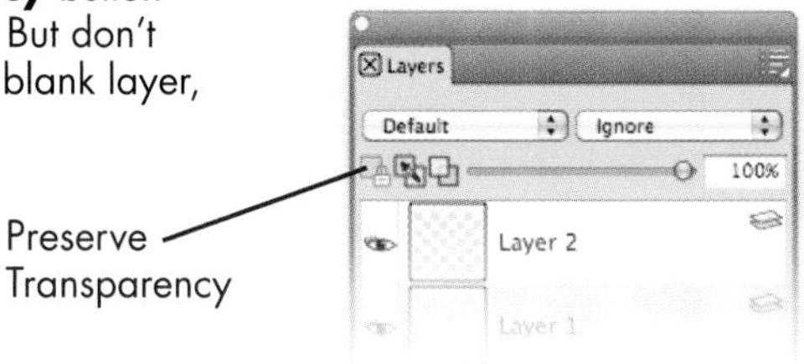

Preserve
Transparency

Figure 10.10
Lock the transparency.

I ended up with *over a hundred layers!* You might wonder how I know which one I want to go back to and select in the list on the **Layers** palette when I have so many of them. Although you can individually name the layers, it takes extra time. The secret is to make sure you have turned **Auto Select Layer** on in the **Property Bar** for the **Layer Adjuster** tool, shown in Figure 10.11. Once you have done this, just clicking on any shape in your picture with the **Layer Adjuster** will automatically activate the correct layer. Figure 10.12 shows preliminary shading of Lincoln's face.

Auto Select Layer

Figure 10.11
Auto load.

Figure 10.12
Honest Abe.

Details, Details!

Besides shading shapes with the **Airbrush**, I also add textures or lines to some of them. I like to use the **Photo Brush Diffuse Blur** variant to create some textures, such as the highlights on Lincoln's hair and beard and to roughen the edges of some shadows such as on his ear.

Painter comes with a terrific variety of brushes, but you can also customize them for even more possibilities. I have a modified version of the **Acrylic Captured Bristle** variant that I used to put the wood grain on the log crib, shown in Figure 10.13. To make the brush have clearer individual bristles, I used the **Brush** control panel for **Static Bristle** and set the controls as shown in Figure 10.14. Figure 10.15 shows the dab and stroke of the default **Captured Bristle** brush, as well as my custom version. You can save custom variants by choosing **Save Variant** from the **Brushes** menu. Just give it a new name so it doesn't replace the **Default Variant** in your brush library.

I made some textured lines with the **Chalk and Crayons Sharp Chalk** variant. This brush is set to be **Grainy**, making it sensitive to **Paper** grain, so it makes a nice rough mark when you use a rough **Paper**.

Figure 10.13
Log texture.

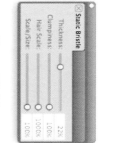

Figure 10.14
Static Bristle settings.

Figure 10.15
Static and ecstatic bristles.

I added lines to the characters' hair with the pen tool, but rather than turning them into selections, I just left them as **Strokes** and adjusted their thickness in the **Set Shapes Attributes** box accessible in the **Shapes** menu and shown in Figure 10.16. I then chose the **Convert To Layer** command from the **Shapes** menu or the **Property Bar** to turn them into pixels instead of a selection. This allowed me to soften them using the Photo Brush, this time set to **Blur**. This is also how I did the "motion lines" behind the hatchet.

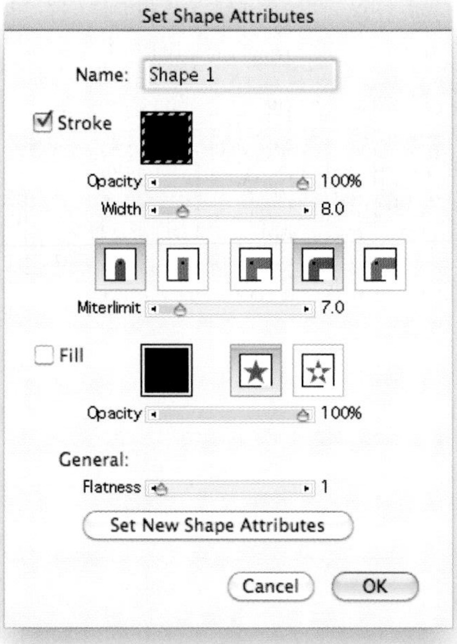

Figure 10.16
Stroke on, Fill off.

I added some texture to Washington's hair by using one of Painter's **Papers**. I love the way these work. Painter lets you import **Legacy Paper Libraries** from older versions you might have. The one I chose was called **Rapunzel** (that seemed appropriate). I inverted it using the button on the **Papers** panel. This made it dark lines instead of light ones, as shown in Figure 10.17.

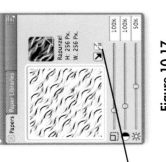

Invert

Figure 10.17
Invert paper.

I selected the hair layer and then made a new **Gel Method** layer above it so the texture would be transparent. I changed the **Digital Airbrush's Subcategory** from **Soft Cover** to **Grainy Hard Cover** using the **General Brush** control panel, shown in Figure 10.18. This makes the brush apply the texture instead of spraying smoothly. Figure 10.19 shows the effect.

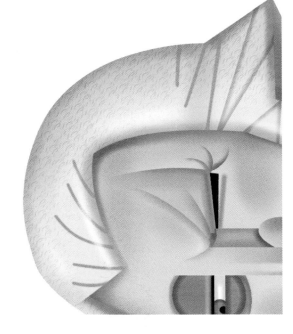

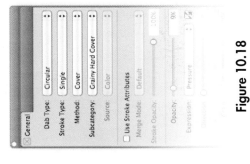

Figure 10.18
From soft to grainy hard.

Figure 10.19
It's a wig.

Drop Everything!

When I'm all through, I make another copy by choosing **Save As** from the **File** menu. With this copy I **Drop All** the layers to the canvas so I have a smaller file that can be sent to a client or easily placed in another document if necessary. Of course I deleted the original sketch layer since I no longer need it.

This technique takes some practice and patience. I spent at least 15 hours on this piece in several different work sessions. If you're interested in working in a similar manner, you might want to start with a simple image until you get the hang of it. Perhaps try a single character's face as a beginning.

Automated Portraiture

After spending time letting Stewart do all the work, let's sit back and make Painter do most of the work. I generally prefer to apply my own brushstrokes one at a time, but I'll make an exception for the amazing **Auto-Painting** feature. This allows Painter to create a cloned painting based on the brush variants you choose, and a few other parameters.

Open **Martin.jpg**, from the **People > Heads** folder, or use another portrait photo if you prefer. Enhance the photo's color by choosing the **Classical Color Scheme** in the **Underpainting** panel. Figure 10.20 shows the enhanced color. Use **File > Quick Clone** and turn off tracing paper.

Figure 10.20
Colorful Martin.

Get Smart

Open the **Auto-Painting** panel and check both the **Smart Stroke Painting** and **Smart Settings** boxes, as shown in Figure 10.21. **Smart Settings** will automatically adjust the size, length, and pressure of strokes in areas of greater detail. With both of those features enabled none of the other options are available, except the speed slider.

Now choose either a **Cloner** variant or any other brush with **Clone Color** enabled in the **Color** panel. Adjust the Speed slider as desired, press the **Play** button, and watch what happens. When you like what you see, press the **Stop** button. I used the **Sargent** brush from the **Artists** category for the result shown in Figure 10.22.

Figure 10.21
Smart boxes checked.

Figure 10.22
Smarty Marty.

Semi-Automatic

You'll have more control (and more fun!) if you uncheck the two Smart boxes and choose from the list of stroke styles now available in the panel. Make a fresh **Quick Clone** of Martin, and try using a **Splat**, **Scribble**, **Hatch**, or **Circle** from the stroke list. Press Play and let Painter apply strokes for just a few seconds. If you don't like the result, use the Undo command. Switch to another stroke from the list and press Play again. For maximum variety, change to another **Cloner** variant from time to time. I used **Clone Color** with both the **Sargent** brush and **Acrylic Captured Bristle** to develop another portrait of Martin. An early stage, shown in Figure 10.23, is dominated by **Swirly** strokes made with the multi-colored **Captured Bristle** variant. Figure 10.24 shows numerous **Scribble**, **Squares**, and **Circle** strokes added. It's not a bad abstract painting at this stage.

Figure 10.23
Get a swirly.

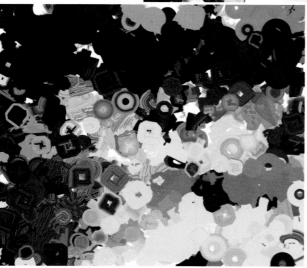

Figure 10.24
Scribbles and circles and squares.

I wanted to soften some of those geometric shapes, so I "cheated" by applying several strokes with the **Water Rake Blender** by hand. That stage appears in Figure 10.25.

Figure 10.25
Raked by hand.

At this point, the background looks fine, but I'd like to get Martin's likeness to emerge a bit more, so I make a loose **Lasso** selection around his head and apply **Simple Sketch Line1** strokes with the **Sargent** brush. The effect, shown in Figure 10.26, is a bit prickly, but the whole painting seems to work. There is enough of a likeness, especially if you stand way across the room, and there is an interesting variety of strokes, colors, and contrast.

When Worlds Kaleid

New in Painter 12 are the **Mirror** and **Kaleidoscope** painting modes, which allow you to draw and paint with horizontal, vertical, or radial symmetry. The **Kaleidoscope** feature provides as many as 12 planes for complex repeats. Figure 10.27 shows simple "snowflake" effects resulting from making just a few strokes with an increasing number of symmetry planes. I used a **Liquid Ink** variant for these, mostly because I hardly ever use **Liquid Ink**.

Figure 10.26
Painter can't tell when you're done.

Figure 10.27
Using 3, 5, 8, 10 and 12 planes.

The Other Kaleidoscope

Painter also has a Kaleidoscope effect, grouped with the other **Dynamic Plugins**, whose icon appears at the bottom of the **Layers** palette. This plug-in allows you to make a small square that can be moved around on any image, creating kaleidoscopic effects that update as you move the square.

You'll explore Kaleidoscope painting using the **Radial Hands** image shown in Figure 10.28. This image already has radial symmetry, so you've got a leg up.

Figure 10.28
Give me a hand.

Choose the **Kaleidoscope** tool, which shares a space with the **Mirror Painting** tool. The **Property Bar** options, shown in Figure 10.29, let you determine how many sections your canvas will be divided into. You can move the center point and change the angle of the segments at any time. The **Symmetry Planes** are bright green by default, but you can change that, too. Toggle the visibility of the planes as it suits you, and use the on/off toggle to switch to normal painting mode and back again.

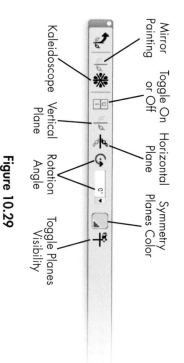

Figure 10.29

Kaleidoscope options.

Choose three planes (which makes six segments) and place the center of the **Planes** at least an inch away from the center of the image, to enhance variety and avoid absolute symmetry. Make a new **Layer** in **Gel** mode so you can see the underlying image and keep it protected from changes. Use **Fine Point Pen** and trace the outline of the hand at the upper right. Figure 10.30 shows the **Planes** plainly, as well as this first stage of **Kaleidoscope** drawing.

Switch to the **Real 6B Soft Pencil** variant and draw an outline of the hand at the 10:00 position with a warm brown color. For some bold strokes, choose the **Thin Smooth Calligraphy Pen** to outline the hand at the one o'clock position. Figure 10.31 shows the results, with **Canvas** visibility turned off.

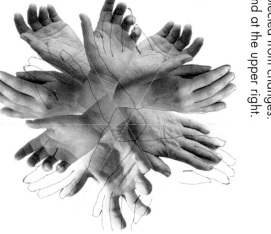

Figure 10.30

Six of one.

Variations

I encourage you to choose different colors, **Pen** and **Pencil** variants, and hands to outline. Every choice you make will be multiplied by six.

Figure 10.31
Half a dozen of the other.

The next stage, shown in Figure 10.32, includes outlining the hand at the lower left with a Pencil in red and scribbling around the outline to create a silhouette. The offset center results in quite a few lines disappearing off the edges of the image.

Figure 10.32
Scribble a silhouette.

Make a new layer for the next stage, so you'll have some composite options later on. Outline the hand at the lower right on this layer, as shown in Figure 10.33.

Back to the previous layer, add more scribbles in yellow-orange. The additional red scribble made at the top of the image didn't look good in the areas where it was mirrored, so I toggled the kaleidoscope effect off and used an eraser to carefully eliminate the repeats I didn't want. This stage appears in Figure 10.34.

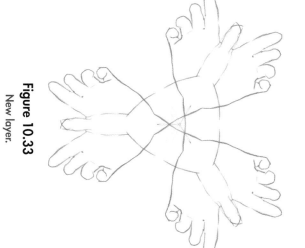

Figure 10.33
New layer.

Figure 10.34
More kaleidoscribbling.

The final art, shown in Figure 10.35, includes the original photo composite. I used **Darken** for the **Composite** method of the main layer. I tried a few combinations for the second layer, ending up using **Screen** method, which has a luminous effect. The result is a bit like a mandala, but I suppose we should call it a *Handala*.

What's Next?

That's totally up to you! Go back and revisit some of the projects, using different source images or techniques. Explore some of Painter's features I didn't get around to showing you. Use Painter in your professional work, or for personal fulfillment. But, above all, have fun with it.

Figure 10.35
Put your hands together!

A Fundamentals and Beyond

In these few pages, you'll find some useful recommendations for continuing with digital painting after you're finished with this book. But first, there are a few things to discuss that will get you off on the right foot, if it's not too late.

Pixels versus Vectors

Painter and Photoshop are pixel-based. The word "pixel" is short for picture element, using the common abbreviation "pix" for "picture." Each pixel represents a tiny colored dot or square, and with enough of them lined up horizontally and vertically you'll get the picture. Resolution, measured in pixels per inch or ppi, tells you about the quality of the image. A resolution of 300 ppi has a much finer grain and more detail than the same image at 72 ppi. Resolution is especially important when images are prepared for printing. Pixel-based (also called raster or bitmap) images must include information about the color and location of every single one of those pixels. Depending on the dimensions and resolution, there can be thousands of such pixels in an image, resulting in hefty file sizes. For example, a Painter or Photoshop file that's 8"×10" at 300 ppi weighs in at 20MB. The larger the file size, the more RAM is needed and the harder your computer has to work.

By contrast, vector-based programs like Flash and Illustrator are resolution independent and have the advantage of smaller files, because the image elements this time are not pixels but paths with simple fills and strokes (outlines) that can be stored as mathematical instructions. By their nature, vector-based images tend to have hard-edged lines and flat color fills, whereas pixel-based graphics can have the kind of variation (called continuous tone) seen in photos and traditional paintings. Working with pixels is intuitive and natural, in my opinion, but it takes considerable practice to get skilled at placing the anchor points and adjusting the curves that make up vector shapes.

What's Dot?

When you see resolution described in dpi, or dots per inch, the reference is for printed output rather than video display. The dpi measurement of a printer usually needs to be quite a bit higher than the ppi measurement of a video screen in order to produce output of similar quality.

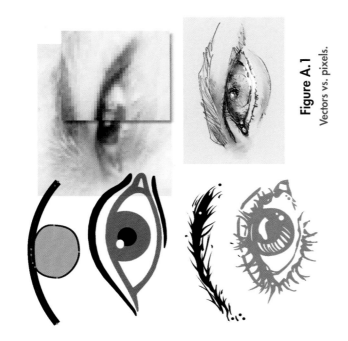

Figure A.1
Vectors vs. pixels.

These eyes show you the difference between pixels and vectors rather dramatically. The photo is zoomed in so you can see some pixels up close and personal. The drawing includes some smears with a Blender variant—smearing can only be done when you're working with pixels. The eyes on the left were all made with vector shapes, and have hard edges. There are pros and cons to each approach, and you don't have to restrict yourself to just one. If you're not sure which category you prefer, ask yourself if you'd rather have precision or instant gratification. Do you like being able to create clean, sharp lines or juicy, smeary ones? I knew I was a pixel-packin' mama from the start!

The Best of Both Worlds

Pixel pushers can have access to some of the benefits of the vector world. In the Presidents' Day cartoon demo by guest artist Stewart McKissick (in Lesson 10, "Special Projects"), you saw Painter's **Shapes** feature in action. Using **File > Acquire**, you can open Adobe Illustrator files that are in AI (Adobe Illustrator) or EPS (encapsulated postscript) format, and see each shape in the **Layers** palette. When you save your image these vector elements must be converted to pixels (or *rasterized*, which sounds much more exotic).

Nice Save!

I just mentioned two file formats used by vector images: AI and EPS. Here's a list of the most basic file formats used by Painter and other pixel-based applications, along with hints on how to choose the best one for your purposes:

- **RIFF (Raster Image File Format):** This is Painter's native format, and images you create in Painter are automatically saved as RIFF files. You need this file format to preserve elements unique to Painter, such as **Dynamic, Watercolor,** or **Liquid Ink** layers. RIFF is also necessary for the **Iterative Save** function. Other applications do not recognize RIFF files.

- **PSD (Photoshop Document):** If your Painter image has default layers (not specialized layers, such as **Dynamic, Watercolor,** or **Liquid Ink**), and you want to switch easily between Painter and Photoshop, use the PSD format. Painter's masks will be preserved as Photoshop channels. However, not all of Painter's composite methods have equivalents to Photoshop blending modes, and text layers will not survive the transition.

- **TIFF (Tagged Image File Format):** This popular format will not preserve layers, dropping them all into the background. One mask can be saved if you use the **Save Alpha** check box. (*Alpha* is Photoshop's term for additional channels created from saved selection masks.)

- **JPEG (Joint Photographic Experts Group):** A very handy format for compressing an image file to make it load quickly on a website or transmit quickly as an email attachment. This compression is *lossy*, meaning the quality of an image will suffer if it is compressed over and over or if low quality settings are used. Be sure to save a copy of your image in another format that will keep its quality intact.

- **GIF (Graphics Interchange Format):** This is the option specifically designed for most non-photographic images used on the web. Colors are reduced to 256 or fewer, and you have several choices for minimizing file size. An ideal format for small animated images on the web.

- **PNG (Portable Network Graphics):** Using a lossless compression method, this format is superior to GIF for transferring images on the Internet. For one thing, PNG allows portions of an image to be transparent. Painter 11 was the first version to be PNG-able.

- **TARGA (Truevision Advanced Raster Graphics Adapter):** This was the native format of the first graphic cards for IBM-compatible PCs to support high-end color display. The compression method used in Targa images performs poorly when compressing images with many color variations, such as digital photos, but works well for simpler images.

- **BMP (BitMaP):** On the Microsoft Windows OS, this is a Raster graphics image file format used to store pixel-based images independently of the display device.

- **PCX (Personal Computer eXchange):** The native file format for PC Paintbrush, developed by the now-defunct ZSoft Corporation. It has been succeeded by more sophisticated image formats, such as GIF, JPEG, and PNG.

Running the Gamuts

Advanced color theory and pre-press technology are beyond the scope of this book, but a few basic color concepts will help you get your bearings. Here are the color terms used in this book, and a few more for good measure.

- **HSV (Hue, Saturation, Value):** *Hue* is a position on the spectrum. The words *red, orange,* and *green* refer to hues but are very inexact. You need to know how pure the color is (*saturation*) and how bright or dark it is (*value*). Other terms for value are *brightness, lightness,* and *luminosity,* all of which are used in Painter in various contexts. The right portion of Figure A.2 shows HSV values displayed as numerical settings for a specific blue in the Color palette.

- **RGB (Red, Green, Blue):** The RGB color model is additive, involving colors emitted from a light source. This color space is useful for describing colors on your monitor. The left portion of Figure A.2 shows the current color with its Red, Green, and Blue components indicated.

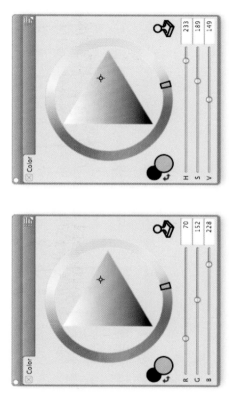

Figure A.2
RGB and HSV.

■ **CMYK (Cyan, Magenta, Yellow, blacK):** This color space is subtractive, involving reflected color from a mixture of paints, dyes, or inks. Painter does not use the CMYK color space.

■ **Gamut:** The entire range of colors available in a given color space. RGB has a larger gamut than CMYK, especially for highly saturated colors. This explains why some colors that look great on your monitor don't look so good in print.

Painter provides a color management feature, available in the **Canvas** menu. The settings, shown in Figure A.3, include a number of options for assigning and converting to color profiles. Your choices depend on your purpose, such as the kind of printing you plan to do. You might need to ask an expert for advice. If you need to provide a CMYK file for print work, the image will have to be opened in Photoshop and converted to that color space, using **Image > Mode.**

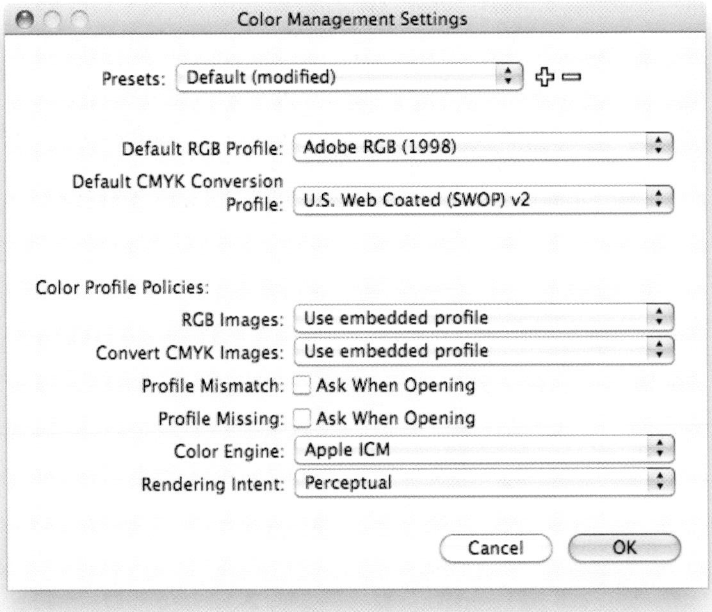

Figure A.3
Color Manager.

Take Two Tablets and Call Me in the Morning

Actually all you need is one tablet, no matter how many computers you may have. If you're shopping around for a graphics tablet, I'll make things easier for you. Wacom Technologies is the only manufacturer to consider. They make a range of tablets in several sizes, for every budget and work situation. Starting with the entry-level Bamboo series all the way to a Cintiq, which is actually a monitor you can draw on. My personal choice is the mid-range Intuos4 model and my preferred size is the very portable 6" × 9".

The Wacom website, www.wacom.com, is as user-friendly as can be, offering you help in deciding which tablet is best for you, downloads for updating drivers, and technical support. They even host a community of photographers, illustrators, designers, and mixed media artists for discussions, competitions, and posting of images. It goes without saying that Wacom has a Facebook presence.

Your tablet should automatically be in "pen mode" after you install the driver software, so every point on the tablet has a matching point on the screen. When you move your pen over the tablet, the cursor moves in precisely the same way on the screen. Where you touch your pen tip to the tablet is a click. If you need to customize the mapping relationship, use the Wacom **Tablet** preferences. The section for mapping is shown in Figure A.4. This is the Mac version, found in **System Preferences**. The way to find this control panel on the PC is as follows: choose **Start > All Programs > Wacom Tablet > Wacom Tablet Properties**. The default configuration is full screen mapped to full tablet, but you can designate only a portion of the screen (or tablet) for point-to-point matching.

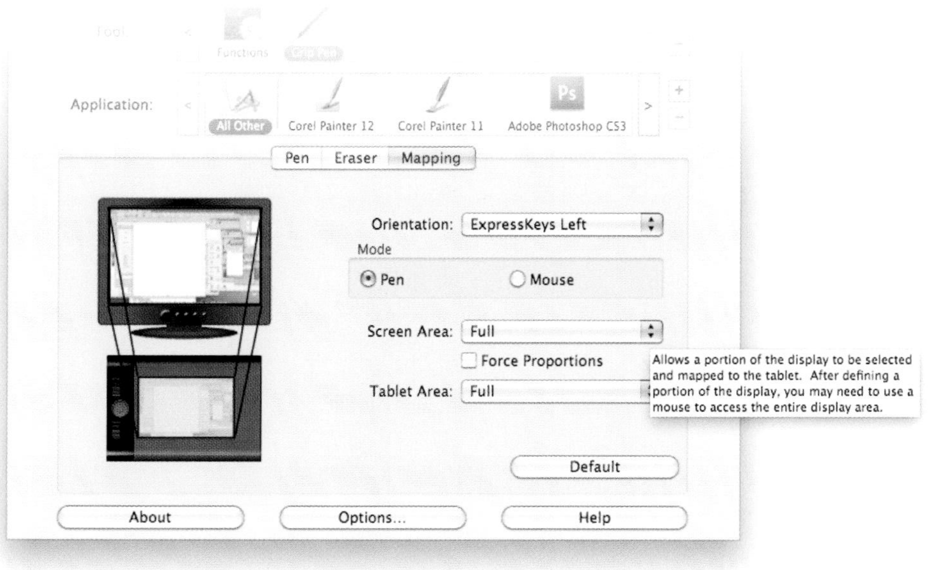

Figure A.4
Tablet mapping.

Figure A.5 shows the Wacom control panel with options for the Pen selected. The lever on the pen barrel has two positions that are capable of double-click and right-click actions by default, but each can be programmed for a variety of other purposes. I routinely disable the lever, because I don't want to be annoyed by accidental clicks or pop-up menus as I manipulate the pen while I work.

Notice the upper section of the panel, where you can specify which tablet or stylus you are using. You can also add applications and create custom settings for each one.

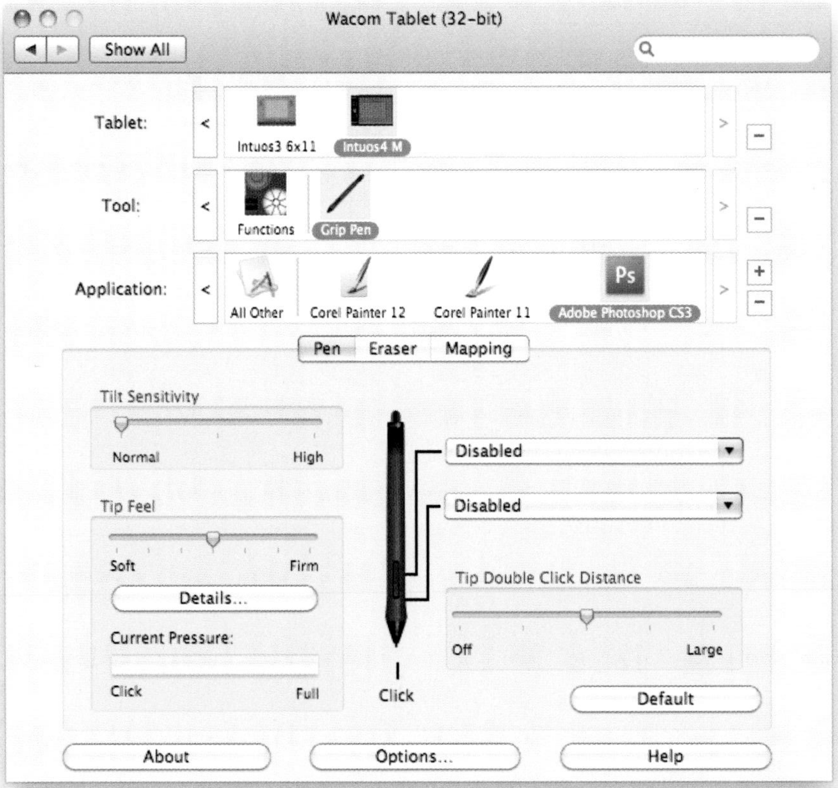

Figure A.5
Pen pointers.

Some of the many customizing options for the Intuos4 tablet are shown in Figure A.6. When you click the **Functions** icon in the **Tool** field, options for programming tablet buttons are available. This view shows the default functions for the **ExpressKeys**, along with menus that allow other choices for each button. Additional displays for the **TouchRing** and **Radial Menu** button are not shown. Intuos4 offers a wide variety of special options and features. I suggest you get accustomed to using the default functions for each **ExpressKey**. The **TouchRing** is a handy way to zoom in and out and to change brush sizes on the fly.

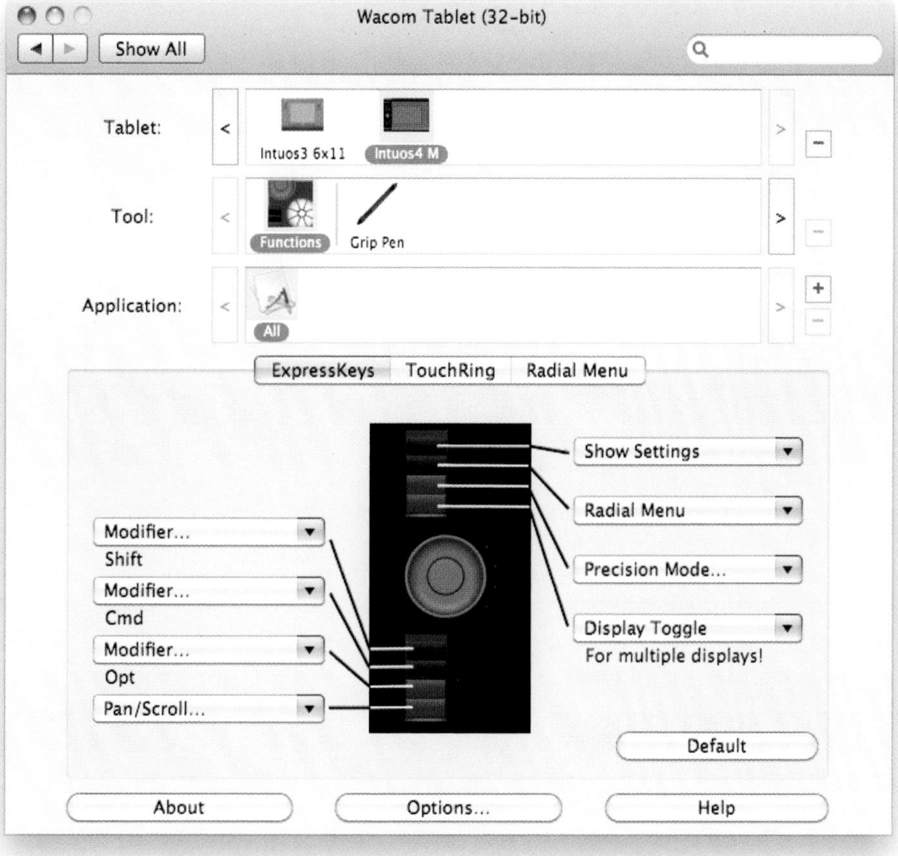

Figure A.6
Don't forget your keys.

Use a Shortcut

Another excellent way to increase speed and efficiency (if you're into that sort of thing) is to learn the keyboard shortcuts for the most frequently used commands. Some of these are specific to Painter, but most are used by all programs, so you might know them already. A couple of modifier keys are different for Mac and PC users. On the Windows platform, the **Control** key corresponds to the **Command** key on a Mac (that's the key with the Apple logo and the thing that looks like a four-leaf clover with an eating disorder). The **Alt** key on a PC is the equivalent of the **Option** key for Mac users. There are a few other differences, like **Delete** serving the same purpose as **Backspace**.

Menu Command	Mac	PC
File > New	Cmd+N	Ctrl+N
File > Open	Cmd+O	Ctrl+O
File > Save	Cmd+S	Ctrl+S
File > Save As	Shift+Cmd+S	Shift+Ctrl+S
File > Iterative Save	Option+Cmd+S	Alt+Ctrl+S
File > Close	Cmd+W	Ctrl+W
File > Print	Cmd+P	Ctrl+P
Edit > Undo	Cmd+Z	Ctrl+Z
Edit > Redo	Cmd+Y	Ctrl+Y
Edit > Copy	Cmd+C	Ctrl+C
Edit > Paste	Cmd+V	Ctrl+V
Select > All	Cmd+A	Ctrl+A
Select > None (Deselect)	Cmd+D	Ctrl+D
Select > Hide/Show Marquee	Shift+Cmd+H	Shift+Ctrl+H
Window > Zoom In	Cmd+ **+** (plus sign)	Ctrl+ **+** (plus sign)
Window > Zoom Out	Cmd+ **−** (minus sign)	Ctrl+ **−** (minus sign)
Window > Zoom to Fit	Cmd+0 (zero)	Ctrl+0 (zero)
Window > Screen Mode Toggle	Cmd+M	Ctrl+M

Get Off My Intellectual Property!

Here's some free legal advice, and I assure you it's worth every penny.

If you scan images printed in books or magazines or search the web for digital pictures, be aware that such items might be copyright protected. That's not a problem unless you want to publish your edited versions. Copyright law gives the original creator of an image all rights to it, including derivations thereof (or is it "wherefrom"?). How much would you have to change an image to make it legally your own and not just a derivation? Are you willing to go to court to find out?

When it comes to using the likeness of a celebrity, things can get complicated. Are you infringing on the copyright of the subject or the photographer who created the photo? Maybe both. Famous people have the right of publicity to prevent others from making money with their likeness, even after death. On the other hand, ordinary folks have the right to privacy, so you need to get a "model release" signed before you can legally publish their faces.

There are exceptions to copyright protection, called fair use. For example, you can publish doctored images of famous people for satirical purposes. Copyright expires 70 years after the death of the creator (last time I checked), after which the image becomes public domain, so anything goes. An image like the Mona Lisa is way in the public domain, even though the actual painting is owned by the Louvre in Paris. Ownership of a piece of art is completely separate from usage rights. The images made available to you on the website that supports this book are provided only for your personal use in working the projects. All other rights are reserved by the copyright holders.

Resources

This section suggests sources for more training, images to play with, media to print on, and even places to display your work so that other digital painters can view it.

There is instant access to online tutorials and the Painter community from your **Help** menu. Choose **Help > Tutorials** to learn from such Painter luminaries as John Derry, one of the original creators of the program. **Help > Painter Videos Online** takes you to an in-depth series on custom workspaces, presented by several Painter Masters. These include "Concept Sketching," "Creativity," "Watercolor," and making the transition from Photoshop to Painter.

Go directly to the Corel website and look under **Resources > Newsletters > Painter Canvas** where you can sign up for this free monthly electronic "forum" for Painter aficionados to learn new tips and techniques, to share and download custom brushes and product freebies, and to discuss all things Painter."

When you launch Painter, don't be too quick to dismiss the welcome screen, shown in Figure A.7. Clicking on **Get Workspaces** brings you to a page on the Corel website that offers not only workspaces but also extra content for downloading—**Brushes, Paper Textures, Patterns, Nozzles,** and more.

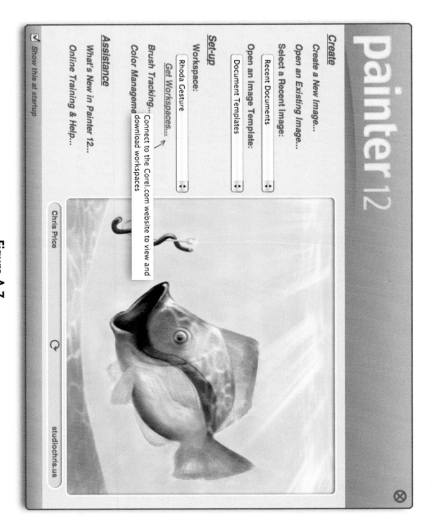

Figure A.7
You're welcome!

Finding Images

If you enjoyed working with the stop-motion photos by Muybridge in Lesson 8, "Drawn from Life," you might want to buy the entire collection from Dover Publications. There are two slim volumes—*Muybridge's Animals in Motion* and *Muybridge's Human Figure in Motion*—that provide not only a printed catalog showing each photo sequence, but all images on a CD as electronic clipart. For only $14.95 ($22.50 Canadian), you get enough raw material to keep rotoscoping for years. Are these images royalty-free and in the public domain? You betcha—Muybridge died in 1904.

You'll probably want to shoot most of your own source photos, but when you need a variety of images or something unusual in a hurry, use the Internet. If you don't mind low resolution, and are careful about possible copyright issues, you can use Google's search engine. When you get to the Google home page at http://www.google.com, click on **Images** instead of **Web** at the top of the screen and type what you're looking for. This is a great way to get visual references for accuracy, or just browse for ideas.

There are commercial online sources for high-quality stock photography. They generally require payment of fees for specified usage and their target market is professional designers and illustrators. If you want a lot of images, those fees can really add up. For stock images with a liberal licensing agreement at bargain prices, my vote goes to ShutterStock.com. It's easy to use their Boolean search engine to find what you need quickly and, best of all, you can subscribe for a relatively small fee, considering the volume of images you'll get. One month of this service costs $249 last time I checked, and allows you 25 images per day or a total of 750 photos for the month. That's about 33 cents per image. Other companies can charge $200 for a single photo! Check it out at http://www.shutterstock.com.

Consider using your older (analog) photos. Take old snapshots out of the family album or the shoebox and digitize them. A basic scanner is pretty cheap, and is a handy device to have around. If you want to digitize images found in books or magazine, your scanner should have a **Descreen** feature. This is needed to prevent an unsightly *moiré pattern* from the halftone dots used in process printing. Published images are almost certainly copyright protected; not a problem if you're just using them in the privacy of your own home and with consenting adults.

Color Printing

A good inkjet printer can provide excellent output as long as you use high-quality paper or other media to print on. Ordinary paper is too porous, letting ink spread into the fibers, so images get blurry or muddy looking. Given the gamut limitations that come with the territory, my choice for crisp rich color is glossy photo paper. Epson and HP make it, among others. It comes in various weights and can be glossy on both sides.

For wearable art, consider printing your images on iron-on transfers that can be applied to clothing, hats, or what-have-you. Avery makes inkjet magnet sheets, which I print with several small images. Then I trim them into shapes for some unique refrigerator magnets.

Archival-quality papers are available for fine art printing from your desktop. A great resource is Digital Art Supplies (http://www.digitalartsupplies.com/), where you can find a range of high-end papers, fabric, and canvas. If you plan to print on canvas, you won't need to add an optical canvas texture to your artwork. They offer several beautiful Japanese papers that I use for printing my gesture drawings. Be advised that these folks are based in San Diego and have a somewhat laid-back attitude about customer service.

If you want to print BIG but don't want to invest in a large format printer, order from an outfit like www.imagers.com/poster.html. Visit their website for a price list of poster sizes from 18" × 24" to 59" × 96" printed on photo paper, film, vinyl, or canvas.

Fonts

After using the **Text** tool for a while, you might get a hankering for more exciting typefaces than just the ones factory-installed on your computer. Lots of fonts are available free, or nearly free, for personal and commercial use. They can be downloaded from sites like Larabie Fonts at www.larabiefonts.com. Larabie offers the "Ultimate Font Download"—10,000 fonts for $19.95. Such a deal!

If you need a special font, and are willing to pay a little more for it, there are quite a few possibilities. LetterHead Fonts specializes in rare and unique fonts for artists and designers. Their home page is breathtaking, and browsing this site is pure pleasure; see http://www.letterheadfonts.com. Incidentally, many type houses still call themselves foundries, even though they hardly ever need to pour molten metal into molds anymore.

Fonthead Design, http://fonthead.com, sells distinctive and whimsical display fonts for about $15 each. Several collections of about a dozen fonts grouped by themes, such as Old Writing or Rough and Tough, are sold for about $40 per volume. Fonthead makes HotCoffee, GoodDog and CatScratch, three of my personal favorites, shown in Figure A.8. GoodDog is actually a freebee, as is a set of cartoon face dingbats (small decorative images or symbols) called font heads.

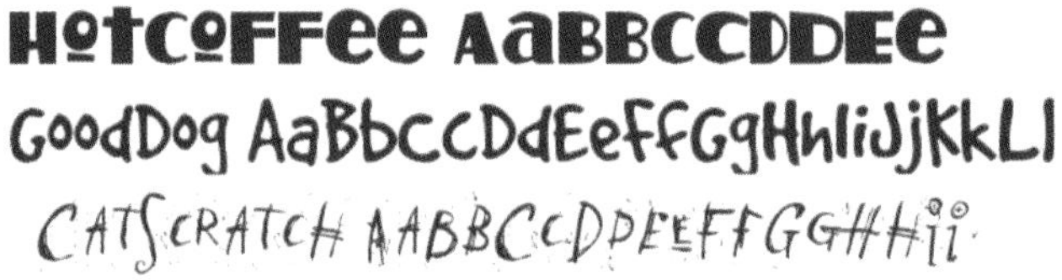

Figure A.8
A dog, a cat, and a cuppa coffee.

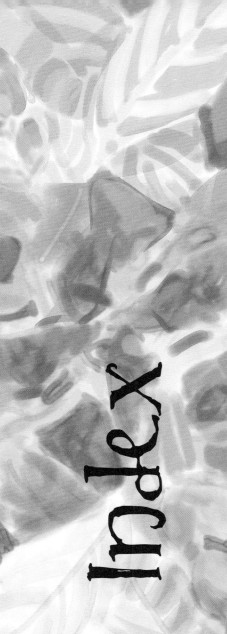

Index

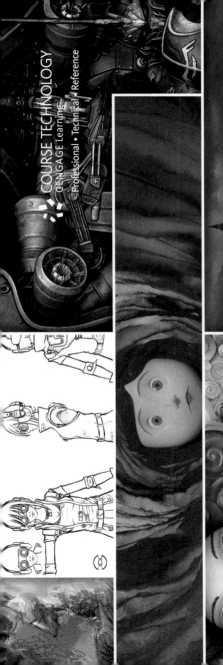

ESSENTIAL SKILLS, INDISPENSABLE BOOKS

Course Technology PTR has the resources you need to master essential graphics and animation software and techniques. Featuring detailed instructions, insight, and tips from industry pros, our books teach you the skills you need to create unique digital art, believable characters, and realistic graphics using Poser, Painter, Zbrush, and more.

**Secrets of
ZBrush Experts**
1-4354-5897-4 • $44.99

Practical Poser 8
The Official Guide
1-58450-697-0 • $49.99

**Digital Painting Fundamentals
with Corel Painter 12**
1-4354-5988-1 • $39.99

Anime Studio 6
The Official Guide
1-4354-5561-4 • $39.99

**Character Development
in Blender 2.5**
1-4354-5625-4 • $44.99

Poser 8 Revealed
The Official Guide
1-59863-970-6 • $39.99

**Photoshop CS5
Trickery & FX**
1-4354-5757-9 • $49.99

**Secrets of
Corel Painter Experts**
1-4354-5720-X • $44.99

**The Advanced Art of
Stop-Motion Animation**
1-4354-5613-0 • $49.99

COURSE TECHNOLOGY
CENGAGE Learning™
Professional • Technical • Reference

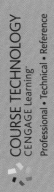

COURSE TECHNOLOGY
CENGAGE Learning™
Professional • Technical • Reference

Like the Book?

Let us know on Facebook or Twitter!

facebook.com/courseptr

t

twitter.com/courseptr